THE MILFORD SERIES
POPULAR WRITERS OF TODAY
ISSN 0163-2469
VOLUME FIFTY-EIGHT

The PRICE *of* PARADISE
The Magazine Career of F. Scott Fitzgerald

by

Stephen W. Potts

Edited by
Paul David Seldis and John Hansen Gurley

THE BORGO PRESS
Twentieth Anniversary, 1975-1995
Post Office Box 2845
San Bernardino, CA 92406
United States of America

* * * * * * *

Copyright © 1993 by Stephen W. Potts

All rights reserved.
No part of this book may be reproduced in any
form without the expressed written consent of the publisher. Printed in the United States of America by Van
Volumes, Ltd. Cover design by Highpoint Type & Graphics.

Library of Congress Cataloging-in-Publication Data

Potts, Stephen W., 1949-
  The price of paradise : the magazine career of F. Scott Fitzgerald / by Stephen W. Potts.
    p. cm. — (The Milford series. Popular writers of today, ISSN 0163-2469 ; v. 58)
  Includes bibliographical references and index.
  ISBN 0-89370-187-4 (cloth). — ISBN 0-89370-287-0 (pbk.)
  1. Fitzgerald, F. Scott (Francis Scott), 1896-1940—Authorship. 2. Periodicals, Publishing of—United States—History—20th century. 3. Authors and publishers—United States—History—20th century. 4. Literature publishing—United States—History—20th century. 5. Short story. I. Title. II. Series.
PS3511.I9Z825 1993   93-344
813'.52—dc20   CIP

THIRD PRINTING

CONTENTS

An F. Scott Fitzgerald Chronology		5
Introduction		9
1.	The Gates of Paradise	13
2.	Spokesman for the Jazz Generation	35
3.	Hitched to the *Post*	55
4.	False Starts and False Endings	77
5.	Pasting It Together	97
6.	The End of a Life, the Beginning of a Legend	115
About the Author		120
Bibliography		121
Index		125

The Price of Paradise

AN F. SCOTT FITZGERALD CHRONOLOGY

1896 Francis Scott Key Fitzberald born on September 24 in St. Paul, Minnesota.

1913 Graduates from Newman Academy, Hackensack, New Jersey, and enters Princeton University.

1917 Citing World War I as the reason, he leaves Princeton before earning his degree to join the army. While at basic training near Montgomery, Alabama, he meets Zelda Sayre.

1919 His first professional sale is published in *The Smart Set*; Scribner's Publishers accepts *This Side of Paradise*.

1920 *This Side of Paradise* is published; his first short stories appear in the *Saturday Evening Post*; he marries Zelda Sayre.

1921 Scribner's publishes his first collection of short stories, *Flappers and Philosophers*.

1922 Publishes the novel *The Beautiful and Damned* and the short story collection *Tales of the Jazz Age*; daughter Frances ("Scottie") is born; moves family to Great Neck, Long Island.

1923 His play "The Vegetable" opens on Broadway; poor critical reviews and low attendance force it to close soon thereafter.

1924 Moves family to the French Riviera; begins another period of publishing in the *Saturday Evening Post*.

1925	Publishes *The Great Gatsby*, which receives a mixed critical response; sales of the novel prove financially disappointing.
1926	Publishes the short story collection *All the Sad Young Men*.
1927	After an unsuccessful stint in California as a Hollywood screenwriter, he moves the family to Delaware and starts his most intense period of writing for the *Saturday Evening Post*, eventually earning $3,500 per story.
1928	First "Basil" stories appear in the *Post*.
1929	The pricetag for a Fitzgerald story in the *Post* rises to $4,000 per; in October, Black Friday's stock market crash launches the Great Depression.
1930	After several months of emotional turmoil, Zelda suffers a nervous breakdown while in Paris.
1931	Fitzgerald returns briefly to Hollywood; the publication of "Babylon Revisited" marks the artistic peak of his *Post* career.
1932	His remuneration for a *Post* story falls to $2,500 per sale; he puts Zelda in an asylum in Baltimore and moves into a house nearby.
1934	Publishes *Tender Is the Night*, which sells slowly; *Esquire* begins publishing pieces under Fitzgerald's name, but the works are actually authored by Zelda.
1935	Publishes the short story collection *Taps at Reveille*; short fiction appears in *Esquire*.
1936	Publishes "The Crack-Up" and two autobiographical essays in the February, March, and April issues of *Esquire*; continues to publish fiction and nonfiction in the magazine through the November edition.

The Price of Paradise

1937 Publishes his last short story in the *Post*; moves once again to Hollywood to become a scriptwriter; embarks on a relationship with Sheilah Graham.

1940 Begins publishing the "Pat Hobby" series in *Esquire*; before completing *The Last Tycoon*, his final novel, he dies on December 21st.

1941 *Esquire* publishes Fitzgerald's last short story.

The Price of Paradise

INTRODUCTION

F. SCOTT FITZGERALD, POPULAR WRITER

Mention the name of F. Scott Fitzgerald to the average American reader, and you will call up visions of the Roaring Twenties, the Boom, Broadway, the Riviera, wild parties, bootleg liquor, romance, and a tragic alcoholic decline. You may even tease out the titles of a few works of fiction: the novels *The Great Gatsby* and *Tender Is the Night* and possibly *The Last Tycoon* and *This Side of Paradise*. It is probable that only determined Fitzgerald fans would be familiar with the best-known short stories, a group including "Babylon Revisited," "May Day," "The Diamond as Big as The Ritz," "Absolution," "Crazy Sunday," and "The Rich Boy." Even Fitzgerald's posthumous reputation among professional scholars has rested largely on the above works and a meager handful of others. In fact, a perusal of the material published for popular and scholarly consumption concerning Fitzgerald and his equally romantic and troubled wife Zelda yields more in biographical detail than it does in critical breadth.

This last observation was if anything more true during the Fitzgeralds' lifetimes. From the 1920 publication of his first novel *This Side of Paradise* to his premature death in 1940, Fitzgerald was never able to shake off the label "Chronicler of the Jazz Age," which often placed his public image above his work. *Paradise* set off the trend for most reviewers; its reflection of the author and his generation seemed more important than its artistic merits, which received little serious attention beyond the reviews of Fitzgerald's acquaintances H. L. Mencken and Edmund Wilson. There is even some question that the book was as widely read as it was notorious: it was on the *Publishers' Weekly* bestseller list for a mere three months, and never rose higher than fourth place. The novels he published subsequently in his lifetime—*The Beautiful and the Damned* (1922), *The Great Gatsby* (1925), and *Tender Is the Night* (1934)—sold increasingly less well; at no time did they earn him near enough money to support his often extravagant lifestyle.

By a wide margin, it was Fitzgerald's work for the popular magazines of his time that provided him with most of his variable income, and it was as a writer of short stories for the magazines, predominantly *The Saturday Evening Post*, that he was best known and most widely read by his contemporaries. In the five-year period that saw the publication of his first three novels, Fitzgerald's byline appeared more than sixty times in the popular press. In the decade between *The Great Gatsby* and *Tender Is the Night*, Fitzgerald published exclusively in periodicals—roughly eighty pieces, fifty of them in the *Post*. It is no wonder that during this decade, fully half of his career, he was considered, and often considered himself, a *Post* writer. From 1934 until his death, Fitzgerald published no more novels (though he was working on *The Last Tycoon* when he died in 1940), but he did publish nearly seventy works of short fiction, expository prose, and verse. This adds up to more then 200 stories, articles, poems, reviews, and public statements published in periodicals during his career, a figure which does not include the nineteen stories classified as lost or unpublished (see Jennifer McCabe Atkinson, "Lost and Unpublished Stories by F. Scott Fitzgerald," *Fitzgerald/Hemingway Annual*, 1971, p. 32-63).

Considering its scope, Fitzgerald's magazine career is probably the most neglected aspect of his work. References to it in critical literature are usually confined to lamentation that so much of Fitzgerald's energy was channeled into relative hack work for the popular press, a point of view often shared by Fitzgerald and his more intellectual colleagues, notably Mencken, Wilson, and Hemingway. The assumption of most scholars, and one frequently backed up by Fitzgerald's own remarks, is that this author "wrote down" to specifications set by the periodicals like the *Post* and its powerful editor George Horace Lorimer. In his critical volume *F. Scott Fitzgerald: A Study of the Stories* (Jamaica, NY: St. John's University Press, 1971), John A. Higgins phrased the issue as follows:

> One major problem in the study of Fitzgerald's stories is determining the extent to which their content and form have been influenced by the requirements or

preferences of the magazine editors to whom Fitzgerald expected to sell them. (p. 14)

Despite his awareness of this problem, Higgins follows the critical consensus by relying on second- and third-hand information about the periodicals in question. For instance, Higgins observes a number of times that Lorimer's *Post* apparently insisted on happy endings, at least up to 1927, a proviso that, according to him and others, limited and debilitated the stories Fitzgerald wrote for the magazine, forcing him to waste his talent on potboiler work. From 1927 to 1935, says Higgins, there did appear to be an alteration in this policy—though no such change was overtly stated—since Fitzgerald stories with less-than-happy endings, such as "Babylon Revisited" and "Last of the Belles," turned up in its pages. It does not seem to have occurred to Higgins, or to any other student of Fitzgerald, that to establish the presence of certain editorial preferences and alterations thereof, one should at least compare Fitzgerald's work with that of his contemporaries publishing in the same periodicals to determine if in fact the so-called "requirements" held true across the board or whether they touch on Fitzgerald in unique ways. If the latter is true, one could reasonably suspect something more particular to Fitzgerald in operation.

This study is an effort to remedy the critical oversight of Fitzgerald's magazine career by examining in detail Fitzgerald's relationship with the readers and editors of contemporary periodicals over the course of two decades. It will provide profiles of the various publications in which Fitzgerald appeared in the course of his career, focusing particular attention on contents and editorial parameters. It will analyze the pieces that Fitzgerald wrote for these periodicals and the readerships they served, toward the end of "determining the extent to which their content and form have been influenced by the requirements or preferences" of the editors. And it will do something else that no other study has done: compare Fitzgerald's work with that of the writers who shared the pages of the popular press with him. In so doing, this study will reevaluate Fitzgerald as artist, professional, and public figure, and place at least one important and under-investigated facet of his career into perspective with its whole.

—Stephen W. Potts
20 April 1993

The Price of Paradise

I.
THE GATES OF PARADISE

Throughout his professional career, F. Scott Fitzgerald tried hard to reconcile two opposing urges: to be an immensely popular writer in his own time, and simultaneously "to be one of the greatest writers who have ever lived," as he told his friend Edmund Wilson (Wilson, "Thoughts on Being Bibliographed," *Princeton University Library Chronicle*, February 1944, p. 54). Something of the same impulse is clear in his early pronouncement, distributed at the American Booksellers Association convention in May 1920, that an author "ought to write for the youth of his own generation, the critics of the next, and the schoolmasters of ever afterward." Herein lies the foremost contradiction in Fitzgerald's work, and perhaps its greatest strength.

Fitzgerald's literary education has been detailed at great length by his biographers. Fitzgerald himself provides the main clues in *This Side of Paradise*, where he gives his own tastes to his hero Amory Blaine. Fitzgerald grew up with the typical youth favorites of his era—Booth Tarkington, Rudyard Kipling, Robert Service, and others less well known today. At Princeton he discovered the Decadents and moderns—Wilde, Shaw, Swinburne, Chesterton, Wells, *et al.* He had entered Princeton, he claimed, to write musical comedies with the Triangle Club; he ended up, under the guidance of fellow Princetonians Wilson and John Peale Bishop, writing poetry and prose for the university's *Nassau Literary Magazine*. It was during his academically troubled stay at Princeton that he finished his first version of *Paradise*, *The Romantic Egotist*. Even more than the published work, it reflects the range of Fitzgerald's styles of the time, containing as it does episodes of romanticism and supernaturalism in the contemporary vein, comic theatre, and decadent verse in the neoaesthetic mode then current in the Ivy League. Indeed, the author's cohorts humorously referred to the

13

novel as "the collected works of F. Scott Fitzgerald." Fitzgerald himself called *Paradise* "a book about Flappers for Philosophers," and while not strictly true the phrase does sum up the breadth of the author's approach.

During the years he was revising and marketing his novel, he also endeavored to place shorter pieces in periodicals. In 1920, with movies still a morally questionable novelty and radio more than a decade away, magazines were the dominate form of mass entertainment, the television of their day. Leading the field by several lengths was the *Saturday Evening Post*, which had been nurtured into that position by its strong-willed editor, George Horace Lorimer. When Lorimer inherited editorial control of the periodical at the turn of the century, it was little more than a stumbling newspaper featuring second-hand material. By World War I he had turned it into a slick, well-illustrated magazine of about 200 pages with subscribers numbering more than two million.

Lorimer knew what the public wanted. Before he assumed the helm of the *Post*, "Most American magazines appealed particularly to women on the accepted theory that men would not buy magazines" (John Tebbel, *George Horace Lorimer and The Saturday Evening Post*, Garden City, NY: Doubleday, 1948). Contrary to the present belief that the *Post* was aimed at midwestern farm wives, Lorimer packaged his periodical for men, particularly the upwardly mobile, middle-class businessman of the Northeast, where America's financial life was based. As a result of this male orientation, his magazine featured

> ...action stories, romances, stories of business; the life stories of successful men of action; articles on economic and political subjects so dramatized that they were at once informing and entertaining; comment on current events; and a modicum of the serious and sentimental poetry countenanced by businessmen of this period. (James Playstead Wood, *Magazines in the United States, Third Edition*. New York: Ronald Press, 1956, p. 152)

In fiction as in articles and editorials, Lorimer avoided the experimental, the intellectual, and the sensational. He did not want his magazine to be confused with the "uplift" periodicals and avoided the inspirational pieces that cluttered them. Neither was he interested in the then fashionable muckraking of a magazine like *McClure's*. Politically, Lorimer spanned the narrow range from Roosevelt Republican to Hoover Republican; he was rigorously pro-business, anti-communist, anti-immigration, and pro-conservation, stances always obvious in the *Post*'s nonfiction departments and occasionally so in its fiction. One of the magazine's specialties was the "business romance," featuring young men who, through honest, persistent pragmatism, solve problems that will capture their financial success, their future security, and, in the process, attractive, sensible women who will make wonderful wives.

In serving so well the tastes of the American bourgeoisie, Lorimer's *Post* received more than its share of criticism from academia, the New York intelligentsia, and even other periodicals for debasing the national literature. Lorimer often insisted that most of it came from the sour-grapes attitudes of those who had been unsuccessful in attempting to publish in the *Post*, and that such criticism was not based on "a fair reading of the weekly and a recognition of the facts" (Tebbel, p. 50). In this view he received resounding support from critic Bernard De Voto, himself a regular contributor of fiction and criticism to the *Post*; he asserted that the "historian is going to recover the surface of American life—at least of middle-class life—much more fully and with less distortion from the slicks than from the novel of our day" (Tebbel, p. 117). Even H. L. Mencken, though he too often attacked the *Post* school of fiction, maintained that blaming the magazine for ruining the writers of the time was "blaming the bull for the sins of all the cows." He added, "It is the largest of the literary Hog Islands, but it is by no means the worst" ("The National Letters," *Prejudices: Second Series*, New York: Knopf, 1920, p. 34-35). In fact, Lorimer serialized a number of Mencken's favorites: Joseph Conrad (*Gaspar Ruiz*), Jack London (*The Call of the Wild*), and Frank Norris (*The Pit, The Octopus*), as well as publishing Theodore Dreiser, Sinclair Lewis, Ring Lardner, and James Branch Cabell. Two of Mencken's most intimate correspondents, Harry Leon Wilson and Joseph Hergesheimer, were *Post* regulars. If the magazine more frequently "published pieces that were tripe, [Lorimer] knew they were tripe" (Tebbel, p. 214).

Fitzgerald's own intellectual qualms about writing for the *Post* were overshadowed by his eagerness, as a budding young professional in 1919, to get into what was, after all, the best-paying, widest circulation market of the era. In the wake of the September sale of *Paradise* to Scribner's, Fitzgerald's letters to his newly acquired agent Harold Ober resounded with anxious inquiry, "Do you think this is *Post* stuff?"

The first periodical that accepted his short fiction, however, was not the *Post* or any of its slick competitors like the *Red Book* or *Cosmopolitan*. Fitzgerald had papered his room with rejection slips from such periodicals when he stumbled upon quite a different marketplace—one that, if not nearly as popular and remunerative, was at least sympathetic to Fitzgerald's self-image. This was *The Smart Set*, a small but notorious monthly co-edited by the aforementioned Mencken, Baltimore critic and iconclast, and Broadway sophisticate George Jean Nathan.

From its founding in 1900, *The Smart Set* had reflected the assumptions and attitudes of the British aesthetic movement of the Yellow Nineties; its pages flourished with verse in the vein of Swinburne and Dowson, Wildean playlets and epigrams, and fiction that tended to the exotic, the escapist, the ironic, and the "naughty." When satire appeared, as it did frequently, it was always social—the comedy of manners—never political; it was not considered "clever" to have political opinions, particularly those of the Left. Mencken and Nathan joined the magazine in 1909, the former as a book reviewer, the latter as theatre critic. Along with Willard Huntington Wright—who would later become mystery writer S. S. Van Dine—they also contributed diatribes against American culture under the pseudonym "Major Owen Hatteras, D.S.O." The newer readers of the World War I generation admired Nathan's worldliness and Mencken's unorthodoxy, and when Wright was forced to vacate the editorship in 1913 the two men were given the job of keeping the financially troubled periodical going.

Though *The Smart Set* had a reputation for publishing the *avant-garde* and the risqué, in fact it specialized in the sort of stories that made James Branch Cabell and O. Henry famous. Although one occasionally found Mencken's critical favorites in the pages—Dreiser, for instance—far more common was the presence of writers like Lord Dunsany and Achmed Abdullah, both masters of the aloof, mannered, cynical, neoaesthetic style. While Mencken the critic was pushing the realists and naturalists—Conrad, Dreiser, Norris, London, and company—Mencken the editor was leaning heavily to the frivolous and entertaining in an attempt to keep circulation figures up. Early in 1915, Theodore Dreiser complained to Mencken of this policy:

> Under you and Nathan the [magazine] seems to have tamed down to a light, non-disturbing period and persiflage and badinage, which now and then is amusing but which not even the preachers of Keokuk will re-

sent seriously. It is as innocent as the *Ladies' Home Journal*. Really the thing is too debonair, too Broadwayesque, too full of "josh" and "kid," like a Broadway and Forty-second Street curb actor. Everything, apparently, is to be done with light, aloof touch, which to me is good but like a diet of souffle. I like to feel the stern, cool winds of an Odyssey now and then. (*The Letters of H. L. Mencken*, Guy J. Forgue, ed., New York: Knopf, 1961)

One can learn something of the range of fiction in the Mencken-Nathan *Smart Set* by glancing at a representative issue. For instance, the February 1915 number featured "The Purple Palette of Life" by frequent contributor Achmed Abdullah. In this long, author-omniscient tale, we watch an unlikely match between an Italian music teacher and a New England heiress break up as the Italian, weary of wooing, moves in with a mistress. His rival for the heiress's affections, an up-and-coming young businessman, spends so much time spying on the Italian he loses his opportunity too. The heiress finds a trace of noble blood in her veins and goes off to marry a titled Englishman, while the Italian abandons his Latin mistress to marry an Irish serving girl. In the end, the jilted young businessman "became also happy and contented, for he acquired large and tainted wealth and glories today in the distinction of the ruling rich: Diabetes." And the author concludes: "So altogether this story is very true to life, and just as it should be."

Equally cynical but far less cheerful is the rarer, gloomier tale that Mencken managed to slip in occasionally amid the frivolity. This genre is represented in the February 1915 issue by Marie Louise van Saanen's novelette "Climbing." An ambitious, profligate, upper middle-class woman badgers her husband into a large investment that soon turns sour, while she, unknown to him, amasses a few thousand dollars in bills at Manhattan shops. Shortly after discovering he has lost everything, he also discovers his wife's bills. An argument ensues, and the husband retreats in apparent resignation. While the wife selfishly waits for his apologetic return, a gunshot resounds from another part of the house.

If this story is an example of the sort of harsh realism Mencken preferred, it more resembles the realism of Stephen Crane and Ambrose Bierce than that of the new wave of writers appearing in the wake of

World War I. In fact, naturalism, like aestheticism, was a literary movement of the 1890s. Though he is thought of as a figure of the twenties, as critic and editor Mencken "belonged to the *avant-garde* of the nineties, not to that of the new generation coming up in the twenties" (Douglas C. Stenerson, *H. L. Mencken: Iconoclast from Baltimore*, Chicago: University of Chicago Press, 1971, p. 221). In this role, however, he performed a great service for American letters by helping to keep alive the *fin-de-siècle* spirit of moral and literary revolt during a stagnant era of sentimentalism in fiction. When American college students and young intellectuals of the World War I era, like Fitzgerald, discovered aestheticism and the moderns of Britain and the Continent, Mencken was there to cheer them on and guide them to the literary revolutionaries of their own country, the Dreisers and Norrises. He and Nathan did manage to advance the cause of literary seriousness despite the forced lightness of their magazine; they introduced James Joyce and Eugene O'Neill to American readers, and published the works of Edna Millay, Ben Hecht, Howard Mumford Jones, Willa Cather, and Stephen Vincent Benét. And the September 1919 issue carried "Babes in the Woods," the first professional publication of F. Scott Fitzgerald.

In overall format at least, *The Smart Set* that introduced Fitzgerald to the public differed little from *The Smart Set* of 1914, the first year of the Mencken-Nathan editorship. Each issue still opened with a novelette, succeeded by short stories, brief lyric poems, usually on romantic or anti-romantic themes, a playlet, several paragraph page-long sketches, numerous epigrams, and the occasional essay. As always, each number ended with a story in French, Nathan's theatre review, and Mencken's book review. An important feature new to 1919 was "Repetition Generale," a loose collection of arbitrary but usually witty judgments by the editors on news items, the arts, personal likes and dislikes, and American society in general.

Thematically, the fiction in the magazine still favored aristocratic romantic comedies; however, Mencken's touch was increasingly evident in the numerical growth of naturalistic tales, usually featuring powerless lower-class types or self-defeating artists and starving intellectuals, and of satires, almost always aimed at Mencken's favorite target, the rising middle-class or "Booboisie." As always, the magazine's attitudes were very clear cut: life was not worth living without cultivated tastes and the money to satisfy them; love was a game, and only aristocrats could play well. American political life was at best a bad farce (Mencken), at worst an irrelevancy that deserved to be ignored

(Nathan); the true aristocrat avoided the crassness of mainstream American social life, with its boosters and Rotarians, its Methodist ministers and prohibitionists. The only tragedy the natural aristocrat could not avoid was age, which felled many a former playboy or wealthy widow in the fiction of *The Smart Set* regulars L. M. Hussey, Mifflin Crane, Thyra Samter Winslow, and Gertrude Brooks Hamilton. These were the writers who excelled in stories of "realism," as Mencken defined it.

In his essay "An Introductory Reminiscence," in Carl Dolmetsch's *Smart Set: A History and Anthology* (New York: Dial, 1966), S. N. Behrman observed that in the World War I era, "ambitious literati could be divided, roughly, into two classes: those with a greater grip on reality, who wanted to write for *The Saturday Evening Post* or *Cosmopolitan* and those, more vaporous, who wanted to write for *The Smart Set*" (p. xix-xx). As we have already noted, Fitzgerald belonged to the first group. All evidence suggests that he initially sold his work *The Smart Set* "only after he was convinced that no other editor uld pay more" (Henry Dan Piper, *F. Scott Fitzgerald: A Critical trait*, New York: Holt, 1965, p. 64). It was widely known among ng writers at that time that one "could send [*The Smart Set*] things couldn't possibly hope to get in anywhere else" (Behrman, p. xxii). e magazine offered low pay, rarely more than fifty dollars a story, had considerable status among the intelligentsia for its reputation of ng "electrifyingly *avant-garde*" (Behrman, p. xxi). The periodical's ob appeal, its aristocratic pretensions, and its collegiate neoaestheticm must have appealed to Fitzgerald, even if the money did not.

The first Fitzgerald pieces to appear in *The Smart Set*—"Babes the Woods" and the playlet "The Debutante"—are self-contained exrpts from *This Side of Paradise*. Published respectively in September d November of 1919, both are slightly different from the final verons of the scenes that would appear in the novel. In the first, the ero, here named Stephen Palms (Amory Blaine in the novel), meets the "speed" Isabelle at a party and comes within a hair of kissing her in a dark parlor before being suddenly interrupted by an influx of party-goers. The episode ends, in *The Smart Set* as well as in the novel, with Isabelle cursing into her pillow. "The Debutante" is the episode which opens Book II of *Paradise*. It details the first meeting of Amory and the baby vamp Rosalind at the latter's "coming-out." In this case the kiss is consummated, with the implication that in winning this goal Amory has lost his heart; the last line is Rosalind's "Poor Amory!"

Earlier versions of both pieces had also appeared in the *Nassau Literary Magazine* during Fitzgerald's undergraduate career.

Naturally the episodes share a number of characteristics. Both take place at smart social functions; that Amory (alias Stephen Palms) is an aristocrat at heart is a fact Fitzgerald makes clear from the opening passage of the novel and throughout. Both focus on a sophisticated love game in which both parties, young though they may be, know all the rules. In both cases the prize seems to be winning the kiss without losing one's head, reputation (for better or for worse), or independence. It has already been noted that upper-class romantic play was a standard motif of *The Smart Set*, and Fitzgerald himself later pointed out that "petting in its more audacious manifestations was confined to the wealthier classes—among other young people the old standards prevailed until after the war" ("Echoes of the Jazz Age," *The Crack Up*, Edmund Wilson, ed., New York: New Directions, 1965, p. 15).

Also typical of *The Smart Set* style is Fitzgerald's aloof, ironic, intrusive presence in the proceedings. The fundamental lack of seriousness with which the characters play at love is seconded by the author-narrator; he remains onstage with his characters, and no matter who is speaking, author included, the epigrams fly thick and fast. These appear even more pointedly and paradoxically Wildean in the *Smart Set* version than in the novel. For instance, immediately under the subheading "Babes in the Woods" in the novel is the line, "Isabelle and Amory were distinctly not innocent, nor were they particularly brazen." In the magazine version the latter half of this reads, "nor were they otherwise." The dramatic dialogue of "The Debutante" can barely proceed at all without some witty remark or epigram, including an oft-repeated early favorite of Fitzgerald's: "a sentimental person thinks things will last—a romantic person hopes against hope that they won't."

In being upper-class comedies on the theme of love-play, in possessing an epigrammatic style and the ubiquitous, obvious presence of the author-narrator, both these pieces merit comparison with light stories of the aristocracy that had long dominated the pages of *The Smart Set*. Since Fitzgerald obviously did not write his excerpts from *This Side of Paradise* specifically for the magazine, the coincidence of style and subject matter must be attributed to coincidental factors, namely to Fitzgerald's and *The Smart Set*'s common roots in the fertile soil of 1890s' aestheticism.

At the time of these first sales, Fitzgerald apparently thought of *The Smart Set* as Nathan's magazine; at least Nathan, representing

The Price of Paradise

the more aesthetic, more frivolous side of the periodical, was the man he believed he had to please. In a letter to his agent Harold Ober in late 1919 he states: "I'm on rather good terms with Mr. Nathan and intend to send him half a dozen little one act plays a year" (*As Ever, Scott Fitz—*, ed. Matthew J. Bruccoli, Philadelphia: Lippincott, 1972, p. 6). In fact, he only submitted two plays, "Porcelain and Pink" and "Mr. Icky." It is clear from both that in originally allying himself with Nathan, Fitzgerald was not only embracing the witty sophistication of the former, but also the whimsicality and triviality of the Broadway stage, by and large another manifestation of aesthetic manner over matter. Nathan's preference for style over substance is clear in his reviews; even in his frequent praise of the young Eugene O'Neill, it was the playwright's poetry he extolled more than his realism.

Though one could find something of Mencken's influence in the occasional naturalistic pieces and middle-class satires, the drama department of *The Smart Set* was thus dominated by wit and whimsy. Fitzgerald's playlets were characteristic. "Porcelain and Pink" (January 1920) features a liberated young flapper in her bath. Although Fitzgerald has been credited with inventing the flapper in fiction, Nathan had been singing her glories in *The Smart Set* since at least 1915. Here she is clever, sophisticated, and quite daring, as she chats through the bathroom window with her sister's boyfriend in a light, lengthy exchange of double entendres. There is much toying with the conventions of the theatre—for instance, as the flapper positions herself to rise from the tub at the play's conclusion "a murmur, half gasp, half sigh, ripples from the audience" before the stage falls dark with a "Belasco midnight," named after the Broadway director of the time known for his spectacular stage effects.

"Porcelain and Pink" is a trivial piece, though not as sophomoric as "Mr. Icky" (March 1920). Subtitled "The Quintessence of Quaintness in One Act," it is a farce without a plot, a satire without a cause, a grab-bag of gags, wisecracks, and inane stage business that fully reflects its collegiate origins in Fitzgerald's contribution to the *Tiger*, the Princeton humor magazine. The framework upon which this silliness is hung is a mock pastoral, featuring a rustic of indeterminate and ever fluctuating dialect who is losing his dozens of children to the conventional lures of the city. Like "Porcelain and Pink," it is not intended to be an actual stage piece. One characteristic stage direction reads: "The curtain goes up and down several times to denote the lapse of several minutes. A good comedy effect can be obtained by having Mr. Icky cling to the curtain and go up and down with it."

While neither of the playlets demonstrates anything but the most fragile and flimsy artistry, Fitzgerald thought them clever enough to include them in his 1922 short story collection *Tales of the Jazz Age*. Within the setting of *The Smart Set*, they represent the lightest of the light, without even the typical touches of mild cynicism visible in "Babes in the Woods" and "The Debutante." Between the appearances of these two playlets, however, the readers of the magazine had seen somewhat better examples of Fitzgerald's work; the February 1920 issue carried two of his short stories—"Benediction" and "Dalyrimple Goes Wrong."

"Benediction" was Fitzgerald's fourth *Smart Set* publication, and like the first three it features a modern, sexually liberated young lady. The story is a much revised version of his undergraduate piece "The Ordeal," and reflects the brief period during which Fitzgerald contemplated becoming America's Catholic writer. In it, heroine Lois Moran, a nineteen-year-old on her way to an assignation with a man who refuses to marry her, stops by the Jesuit cloister where her novitiate brother Kieth resides. Kieth's love for her, the peace and contentment of his dutiful religious existence, and, ironically, his faith in her virtue amid a world of moral decay—a faith which overcomes all his personal doubts—is presented as attractive, though naive. Lois has an epiphany of sorts at the story's climax, when she wrestles with her guilt during mass, a struggle which ends with her fainting. Near the end of the story, Kieth sends her on her way with his blessing in a scene thick with sentiment and irony. The final scene takes place in the telegraph office where the story began, with two clerks musing over the message Lois was about to send but tore up at the last minute, a message which would have permanently cancelled her affair. The reader infers she keeps her assignation.

"Dalyrimple Goes Wrong" has in common with "Benediction" the sort of moral twist a devotee of *The Smart Set* would appreciate. In fact, it is difficult to believe that "Dalyrimple" was written, as Fitzgerald alleged, "with *The Saturday Evening Post* in mind...or...the *Cosmopolitan*" (*As Ever*, p. 5). Significantly, this is the first story Fitzgerald published that uses the characters of the unsophisticated middle class to burlesque some basic tenets of the American credo, a common Menckenian practice. Fitzgerald apparently had not discovered Mencken until December of 1919, some months into his association with *The*

The Price of Paradise

Smart Set. In January 1920 he slipped the critic's name into his final revision of *This Side of Paradise*. It was not long before attitudes and even phrases of Mencken's started turning up in Fitzgerald's fiction and correspondence.

"Dalyrimple" opens with a paragraph of very "smart" aloof cynicism:

> In the millennium an educational genius will write a book to be given to every young man on the date of his disillusion. This book will have the flavor of Montaigne's essays and Samuel Butler's notebooks—and a little of Tolstoi and Marcus Aurelius. It will be neither cheerful nor pleasant but will contain numerous passages of striking humor. Since first-class minds never believe anything very strongly until they've experienced it, its value will purely relative... all people over thirty will refer to it as "depressing."

What follows is a moral tale of dubious morality, in which a young returnee from World War I—the war itself is described in snide, typically Menckenesque terms—comes back to his small town to seek his fortune. Impatient with the dull, low-paying stockroom position he solicits from a reluctant family friend, Dalyrimple takes to burglary to augment his income. The townspeople, and notably his employers, are impressed with the way he is able to save so much money from his meager wage. Dalyrimple is finally introduced to a local politician, who is going to arrange to have him *put* in the state senate. Dalyrimple's eyes are opened to the truth:

> —so life was this after all—cutting corners—cutting corners—common sense, that was the rule. No more foolish risks now unless necessity called—but it was being hard that counted—Never to let remorse or self-reproach lose him a night's sleep—let his life be a sword of courage—there was no payment—all of that was drivel—drivel.

Fitzgerald retained the ironic mode in his next publication in *The Smart Set*, "The Smilers" (June 1920). Like "Dalyrimple," it had been written for the slicks, but its gloomy cynicism suited Mencken's magazine far better. It hangs on a somewhat puny gimmick: the character to whom we are first introduced cannot understand why the people he comes in contact with are always smiling—life, from his particularly sour aristocratic viewpoint, being the miserable condition that it is. Then the story breaks into three separate vignettes, each detailing the hopeless situation of one of "the smilers" of the man's acquaintance.

Though these pieces written for other markets fit the circa 1920 *Smart Set* quite well, there is no evidence that Fitzgerald wrote specifically with the magazine in mind until he began "May Day," which he referred to in correspondence as "that *Smart Set* novelette" (*Dear Scott/Dear Max*, ed. John Kuehl, New York: Scribner's, 1971, p. 29). At this time he was also praising Mencken and Nathan as "the most powerful critic [sic] in the country," and he wanted both of them "hot on my side when my book comes out" (*Dear Scott*, p. 28), referring of course to *Paradise*, which was due out that spring.

Critics seem to agree that "May Day" is one of the more significant of Fitzgerald's earliest short works, even if there is a little disagreement as to its quality. The most striking aspect of the novelette is the interweaving of its separate plots, primarily three. One concerns the decay of Gordon Sterrett, an artist who has been unable to get his career started and who now finds himself heavily involved with alcohol and a cheap woman who is proving expensive, morally and financially. The second plot follows a pair of low-life soldiers, Gus and Carrol, just home from the war, looking for liquor and a good time. The third focuses on Edith Bradin, a flapper, during and after a college dance at Delmonico's. Filling the interstices between these plots is a small assortment of other characters: Henry, Edith's socialist, journalist brother who is attacked by a mob of soldiers that includes Gus and Carrol; Philip (surnamed Cory in *The Smart Set*, Dean in the version published in *Tales of the Jazz Age*) and Peter (Barton in *The Smart Set*, Himmel in *Tales*), two college men who have connections, respectively, to Gordon and Edith and who in the latter part of the story engage in alcoholic shenanigans as Mr. In and Mr. Out.

In fine *Smart Set* style, Fitzgerald's author-narrator opens the story with an overview in mock Biblical prose of the world events that led up to the situation in New York on May 1, 1919. Here as elsewhere in the piece he maintains a typically aloof, clever, cynical stance. He falls silent during the most painful moments of the narrative, withdrawing like an indifferent god and thus underlining the "meaninglessness of life," a common motif in Mencken's naturalism. Sterrett's suicide at the end of the story exemplifies this emotional distancing; in the familiar *Tales* version he shoots himself without authorial commentary. In the original *Smart Set* version, the event is distanced even further; Sterrett merely shows up as an anonymous figure in a sporting goods store, where he buys a pistol amid the casual chat of two dialect characters and departs.

The types the various characters represent would have been recognizable to *Smart Set* readers, especially in the magazine version. There it is apparent from beginning that Sterrett is hopelessly alcoholic, without even the dignity he possesses in the later rendition. He thus belongs to the class of self-destructive artists depicted often by *The Smart Set* regulars like Ben Hecht. The radicals, particularly Henry Bradin, appear more shrill and ridiculous in the magazine, while the soldiers Gus and Carrol are described in terms almost subhuman, as "ugly, ill-nourished, devoid of all except the very lowest form of intelligence." Such attitudes accord with the editors' haughty notions of the unwashed masses and those on the left who would use them as a power base. The college crowd is generally presented as vain, uncaring, and frivolous, though they are exempted from express authorial disapproval. Taken together, the elements of "May Day" demonstrate how quickly and how well Fitzgerald could formulate a thorough understanding of his market and even absorb an entire aesthetic philosophy and adopt it, at least superficially, as his own.

The publication of "May Day" in July 1920 marked the climax of Fitzgerald's association with *The Smart Set*. By this time, *This Side of Paradise* had become a *cause célèbre*, and its author had finally managed to break into the *Saturday Evening Post*. In response to Nathan's pleas for other manuscripts, Fitzgerald would submit only three more pieces to the magazine. "Tarquin of Cheapside," published February 1921, was a revised college story which has Shakespeare commiting rape prior to the writing of "The Rape of Lucrece." "The Far-Seeing Skeptics" (February 1922) simply showcases two of the most cynical paragraphs of *The Beautiful and Damned*, the Fitzgerald novel that shows the greatest influence of both Mencken and Nathan. Finally, in June 1922 *The Smart Set* published "A Diamond as Big as The Ritz," a novelette which he sent to Nathan only after it had made the rounds of the slicks. A cynical fantasy about ultimate wealth, dripping with decadence and irony, it worked well within the old *Smart Set* format. It belongs, however, to the next chapter of Fitzgerald's career.

The young author's first sale to *The Saturday Evening Post* must have been a thrill second only to the sale of his novel. His first *Post* story, "Head and Shoulders," appeared in the 21 February 1920 issue, following a sinister tale of Chinese murderers in San Francisco, a humorous playlet ridiculing marital folly among New York's wealthy, a comic tale of stereotypical blacks, and an article on the destitute of Europe. Fitzgerald's story begins on page sixteen, with a column-long illustration, bounded by two columns of print, of a bespectacled young man peering down a staircase at an attractive young woman, above the caption, "I Hope I Haven't Given You the Impression That I Consider Kissing Intrinsically Irrational."

This light narrative is two-thirds concerned with the unlikely courtship of a Yale prodigy, Horace, and a shimmying chorus girl, Marcia, and one-third concerned with their first year or so of marriage, during which their circumstances turn him, the intellectual, into a trapeze artist and her, the dancer, into a literary sensation. The gimmick here is mild irony—far different from the typical *Smart Set* story. In "Head and Shoulders" no one suffers as a result of the reversal. The story fits comfortably into the *Post* format: an intimate, droll narrative style, the essential decency of the protagonists, their successful romance, the gentle surprise of their crossing careers and even the positive pragmatism of Horace's final reflections: "Trying to chose our mediums and then taking what we get—and being glad." The disproportionate plot—two thirds courtship, one-third comic reversal—would not have troubled the *Post* editors and readers. Given the length of most *Post* stories, plots frequently had a tendency to wander.

One month after "Head and Shoulders," in the 20 March 1920 issue, appeared Fitzgerald's second *Post* publication, "Myra Meets His Family." Like the first story, it is an insignificant piece, with little or no literary value. Fitzgerald did not like "Myra" himself; he told Harold Ober that it was "no good" (*As Ever*, p. 7) and upon learning of its acceptance wrote: "You could have knocked me over with a feather...I never was so heartily sick of a story before I finished it than that one" (*As Ever*, p. 8). Myra is a bored twenty-one-year-old prom-trotter now engaged in a concerted search for a husband. One likely prospect, a rich young man, invites her to his sizable home to meet his family; however, the gloomy mansion and the eccentricities of the aged parents change her mind. On the verge of sneaking away, she discovers the situation is a fake, an extended scheme arranged by the man to test her motives. Remorseful at being found out, he proposes; she accepts, stages a quick ceremony, then abandons him on the honeymoon train. She has arranged a fake wedding and thus had her revenge.

The twist ending was at much at home in *Post* as it was in *The Smart Set*; indeed, it was fairly standard in the short story of the time. Also, one frequently found the "trickster-tricked" motif in *Post* fiction, particularly when the protagonist was the stereotypical shrewd Jew or clever lawyer, like Arthur Train's perennial Mr. Tutt. In fact, such stories could be thought of as the comic face of business romance, in which the spoils go to the smartest, the one who can best play or bend the rules to his or her advantage.

A similar motif shapes Fitzgerald's next two *Post* stories. In "The Camel's Back," published 24 April 1920, an amorous young man, helped by a series of fortunate coincidences, ends up married to the flapperish female who had earlier rejected him. Aided by the sleazy cab driver who shares his camel costume during a "mock" wedding at a masquerade party, the man tricks the woman into remaining his wife. Though as in "Myra" the characters are less than wholly attractive, all is forgiven when matters turn out right in the conclusion. Marriage more or less typified in the *Post*'s romantic comedies what it did in Shakespeare's: the restoration of order.

A better and more believable story is "Bernice Bobs Her Hair" (1 May 1920). It details the rapid sex education of ugly duckling Bernice under the tutelage of her coquettish cousin Marjorie. Ironically, Bernice learns so well she threatens Marjorie, leading the latter to trap Bernice into bobbing her hair, a "fast" act that ruins her looks and her popularity. Bernice achieves a last-minute revenge by surreptitiously clipping Marjorie's long locks. Despite a few moral ambiguities, the reader has no difficulty sympathizing with Bernice's rise, fall, and revenge, yet the narrator's amused objectivity keeps the story comically painless.

The most serious of his 1920 *Post* stories, and the one best received by the critics, is "The Ice Palace." Though sold to the magazine shortly after "Head and Shoulders," it did not appear in print until 22 May 1920. Constructed principally as a contrast of Northern and Southern cultures, it is heavily loaded in favor of the South, no doubt due in large part to the story's roots in Fitzgerald's courtship of Alabama belle Zelda Sayre. The story opens in the sunny, easy-going, fictional Georgia town of Tarleton, with the lazy, flirtatious young Sally Carrol Happer leaning out of an open window toward a local "jelly-bean." From there the narrative moves to the chilly North, where the heroine goes to become acquainted with her Yankee fiancé's family and milieu. Following a series of disillusioning scenes in which she finds the North and its people cold, lifeless, and ultimately loveless, she becomes lost at the climax in the maze of an ice palace built for the winter fair, a monumental symbol of the North and its potential effect on her. The final scene takes her back to her window in Georgia.

Like the other *Post* stories by Fitzgerald above, this one possesses romantic and comic elements, though here the happy ending is a result of breaking off an engagement and turning away from the hardheaded progress ethic of the industrial North. Fitzgerald could get away with this apparent assault on the dominant business orientation of the periodical because of the ambivalence built in to the *Post* pages. In the early twenties, *Post* readers straddled a decade in which an essentially rural country became the world's industrial leader. There was a good deal of nostalgia already for the simpler ways of life being left behind, and sandwiched between the business romances were many stories praising the virtues of rural America: the Deep South, the Midwest, Far West, and "down East" in upper New England. An oft-repeated motif, mirroring that in "The Ice Palace," is having a young man or woman from the urban Northeast visit the countryside, and there find a more honest and decent life that the one they left behind. Often there are two members of the opposite sex involved, one representing the coldness of the city, the other the homely warmth of the country.

With the unself-consciousness of any popular literature, such stories provided a palliative for the vague discomfort many prosperity seekers of the time no doubt felt about the deep-seated inconsistencies between the new America and what seemed, even then, to be the nobler America of tradition. This contradiction is evident as well, from today's standpoint, on Lorimer's editorial page, which urged conservation of the wilderness even while it wholeheartedly endorsed the laissez-faire economic development of the country. These two disparate currents flow together in the frequent adventure tales of frontiersmen and pioneers, where Leatherstocking-style heroes help push back the wilderness in the name of progress even as they exult in its virgin, natural wholesomeness.

If such sentiments underlie the acceptability of "The Ice Palace," they were probably less overtly important to *Post* readers than the charm of the heroine, the sparkle of much of the dialogue, and the neat if somewhat contrived plotting. The same qualities inform Fitzgerald's next *Post* story, "The Offshore Pirate," which climaxed this phase of

The Price of Paradise

his career with the magazine. Published in the 29 May 1920 issue, "Pirate" is considered by more than one critic to epitomize Fitzgerald's popular romances. It is as far from the snide skepticism of *The Smart Set* as one could get, and it sums up in glittering form the romantic attitudes toward youth, money, and love for which Fitzgerald was and is recognized in the popular mind. Its heroine, Ardita, is the consummate flapper: nineteen, attractive, wealthy, rebellious, jazzy, and well-read in such *Smart Set* favorites as Anatole France.

"The Offshore Pirate" is Fitzgerald's most perfect rendition, in this early group, of the *Post* motif of an ornate scheme concocted to test or win an unsuspecting individual. In the stories of other authors, such schemes were often used to prove the mettle of a potential up-and-coming businessman (see, for instance, "Todd's Plunge," by Charles Magee Adams, in the 3 January 1920 number). Fitzgerald has already used such a plot device in "Myra Meets His Family" to expose the motives of a young husband-hunter. In "The Offshore Pirate," the independent-minded Ardita is kidnapped from her father's yacht while on the verge of running away to marry an untrustworthy rake. Her kidnapper identifies himself as Curtis Carlyle, white leader of a band of black musicians, who participate in the crime, and the perpetrator of an armed robbery. During a few days in the idyllic Caribbean hideaway, the two fall in love. When a patrol boat suddenly arrives, all appears lost until Curtis reveals he is really Toby Moreland, the young aristocrat Ardita's uncle wanted her to marry. Thrilled by his imagination and daring, she accedes.

No doubt the average *Post* reader would have found Ardita "'selfish, spoiled, uncontrolled, disagreeable, impossible,'" to quote her uncle. But in every other respect, she is attractive and energetic. Besides, she receives a comeuppance at the hands of her betters, albeit an inviting and satisfying one. In the end, she wins a marriage with a forceful, imaginative, but respectable male of her own class, which coincides with the wishes of her elders. Once again moral order triumphs in the traditional form of matrimony. "Imagination and convention march to the altar side by side," notes Robert Sklar in *The Last Laocoon*; "it is almost archetypal genteel romance" (New York: Oxford, 1968, p. 70).

The prose itself shows Fitzgerald at his most romantic, beginning with the opening sentences:

> This unlikely story begins on a sea that was a blue dream, as colorful as blue-silk stockings, and beneath a sky as blue as the irises of children's eyes. From the western half of the sky the sun was shying little golden disks at the sea—if you gazed intently enough you could see them skip from wave tip to wave tip until they joined a broad collar of golden coin that was collecting half a mile out and eventually would be a dazzling sunset.

Such lavish language has embarrassed a few scholars, moving critic Henry Dan Piper to suggest that it was intended to parody the *Post* romantic style. This is unlikely, however, considering Fitzgerald liked the story enough to recommend it to Mencken; indeed, he later told Mencken that in 1920 he had "thought that 'Offshore Pirate' was quite as good as 'Benediction'" (*The Letters of F. Scott Fitzgerald*, Ed. Andrew Turnbull, New York: Scribner's, 1963, p. 160).

Though "Pirate" stands out as the jazziest of Fitzgerald's early stories, it fit quite comfortably into its surroundings. The 1920 *Post* was full of young men winning their women through persistence and imagination, though usually in more staid fashion. Fitzgerald was also not the first author to portray the modern woman in the magazine's pages, though he painted her somewhat more sympathetically and with more life than his colleagues, if still with a comic distance that did not require the reader to endorse her behavior completely. Fitzgerald, therefore, did not have a monopoly on youth; a number of the *Post* stories of this period featured ambitious young men and attractive young women. Thus, one must regard skeptically Piper's contention that Fitzgerald's stories single-handedly rejuvenated Lorimer's magazine (*F. Scott Fitzgerald: A Critical Portrait*, p. 309; note to p. 74). Though it is true that the illustrations, advertisements, and the stories of the 1920 *Post* increasingly reflected to some small degree "the unconventional attitudes and values described in Fitzgerald's early stories" (Piper, p. 74), the cause and effect is less certain.

The nation, and particularly the northeastern cultural centers to which Lorimer was most sensitive, were quickly discovering that jazz and bobbed hair were not incompatible with business, progress, and the American Way. Fitzgerald was fortunate to have appeared at the right time to become a spokesman for youth, in part "because it was his fortune to publish a season ahead of the others" (Sklar, p. 109), and a spokesman that was not antipathetic to the middle-class majority. In Fitzgerald's earliest *Post* stories, "the young, for all their daring new ways, played their games by prewar sentiments and standard rules. This must have been deeply reassuring to conservative readers of any age, for it implied that inevitable change would come without any great disruption in the eternal continuities" (Sklar, p. 109). The same was true, by and large, of *This Side of Paradise*, as more than one contemporary reviewer noted. As Sklar points out, "the novel was important because it was exemplary, because it carried the news on youth, and the news was good" (p. 111).

Amid this novel's brief season on the best sellers list, Fitzgerald made his last 1920 appearance in the *Post*, in a column or so of autobiographical material under the heading "Who's Who—and Why," a regular feature of the magazine. The essay, published September 18, overflows with the healthy exuberance of youth and success, which explains the boasting and sophomoric cracks that fill it; as Arthur Mizener states in *Afternoon of an Author*, "Fitzgerald is still inclined to throw his hat in the air and shout" (Princeton: Princeton University Library, 1957, p. 83). Such harmless brashness, however, places the author among those quick, capable, boyish heroes that people 1920 *Post* fiction.

Besides *The Smart Set* and *The Saturday Evening Post*, Fitzgerald had one other market in 1920, though it proved temporary and minor. This was *Scribner's Magazine*, one of the quartet of "quality" magazines that carried on the highbrow, genteel tradition of the previous century, the others being the *Atlantic*, *Harper's*, and *Century*. In the early twenties these periodicals continued to represent and endorse prewar standards in literature, philosophy, and decorum. The tone of *Scribner's* is perhaps best demonstrated by Henry Van Dyke, Presbyterian pastor, Princeton English professor, and active propagandist for moral uplift and pro-War patriotism, who was in 1920 contributing a series of inspirational essays entitled "Guide-Posts and Camp-Fires," full of sentimental and sententious Christianity. Much of the non-fiction mixed the informative with the inspirational ("Korea's Rebellion: The Part Played by Christians") or pointed up the magazine's serious literary orientation, with articles on figures like Henry James and Herbert Spencer. Verse was given a prominent place, though it too harked back to the forms and sentiments of the previous century. The fiction ranges from historical romances to contemporary stories of sentiment and gentle humor.

Scribner's Magazine, under editor Robert Bridges, had seen a number of Fitzgerald's stories and poems in 1919 and returned them all. After Scribner's, the publishing house, accepted *Paradise*, Maxwell Perkins—the famous Scribner's editor who discovered Fitzgerald and others—encouraged the author to try again, naturally with the marketing of the novel in mind. Bridges ended up accepting two stories, "The Cut-Glass Bowl" and "The Four Fists." These appeared respectively in the May and June 1920 issues, immediately following the publication of the novel.

Not surprisingly, the Fitzgerald stories in *Scribner's* are "wooden, uninspired but conscientious copies of the more conventional stories of the day—highly moral and heavily plotted, but with no roots in Fitzgerald's own experience" (Piper, p. 65). They certainly lacked the energy and wit of the pieces he was selling to *The Smart Set* and the *Post*. Both pivot on the same device: a solitary, arbitrary symbol that unifies a series of otherwise remotely connected episodes in the lives of single characters. In "The Cut-Glass Bowl," the symbol is the object of the title, which presides over the termination of the heroine's first romance, then her husband's discovery of her affair with a young man, her daughter's mutilation, her husband's alcoholism and the loss of his fortunes, the killing of her son in battle, and her own apparent death at the story's end. "The Four Fists" also announces its catalytic agent in the title. In this case the hero acquires character by being punched in the jaw at four crucial points in his life; in this manner he overcomes rudeness while the freshest boy at prep school, snobbishness in college, selfishness in young adulthood, and hard-hearted materialism as a mature businessman. In both stories the narrator maintains a didactic and frigid distance, uncharacteristic of the author at this stage.

These stories are mainly significant here as a demonstration of Fitzgerald's ability to write for specific audiences. One typical *Scribner's* subscriber, Princeton president John Grier Hibbens, liked "The Four Fists," though he found *This Side of Paradise* shocking and distasteful. To these observations Fitzgerald replied: "I wrote ['The Four Fists'] in desperation one evening because I had a three-inch pile of rejection slips and it was financially necessary for me to give the magazine what they wanted" (*Letters*, p. 462). Fitzgerald would sell nothing more to Robert Bridges, however. In the wake of his novel, he soon discovered he could do much better than the $150 per story *Scribner's* offered, particularly considering its artistic limitations.

The Price of Paradise

At the end of his first twelve months as a paid professional, he had a best-selling novel behind him, as well as eight pieces in the supposedly avant-garde *Smart Set*, six stories in the popular *Post*, and two in the reputable *Scribner's*. He had demonstrated considerable versatility and both artistic and commercial potential. He had also married the girl of his dreams, Zelda Sayre, received money for story options from moviemakers, and been branded the spokesman of his generation and his age. Given such a dramatic start, he would use this momentum over the following years to pursue both his literary and commercial ambitions.

II.
SPOKESMAN FOR THE JAZZ GENERATION

None of the magazines of Fitzgerald's first year would receive as much attention from him over the next half decade. From the end of 1920 through 1926, the author was able to exploit a wide spectrum of temporary and intermittent markets in the popular press. During this period, the busiest of his career, he was much in demand as a writer of fiction as well as social and literary commentary. In addition, articles and interviews concerning both Scott and Zelda Fitzgerald were prominent in the media, advancing them as the archetypal young couple of the decade. As Kenneth Eble observes in his study *F. Scott Fitzgerald*, for "the readers of the time, the Fitzgeralds' lives were rather constantly before them" (Boston: Twayne, 1977, p. 72). Despite this active public life, Fitzgerald managed not only a lucrative magazine career but the writing of two novels—*The Beautiful and Damned* and *The Great Gatsby*—and a Broadway play, *The Vegetable*.

At least in part, Fitzgerald owed much of his income over these years to his agent Harold Ober, who tirelessly arranged contract after contract with periodicals, story options with Hollywood, and frequent loans against future royalties. The first contract Ober negotiated on Fitzgerald's behalf was with *The Metropolitan Magazine*; Fitzgerald would offer editor Carl Hovey his next six stories at $900 each upon acceptance, a rate substantially higher than even the *Post*, at $500 per story, was then paying him. The relative generosity of the offer may have been motivated to some degree by desperation on the part of the *Metropolitan*. Its circulation at this time was miniscule beside that of the magazines with which it competed, general interest journals such as *Collier's*, *Red Book*, and the Hearst twins, *Cosmopolitan* and *Hearst's International*. It was heading rapidly into bankruptcy under the ownership of the colorful Bernarr Macfadden, best remembered now as the creator of such low-brow journalistic genres as the "true" confession magazine, led by his own *True Story*, the "physical culture" journal, and the sensationalist tabloid, typified by his New York *Graphic*. Whereas in other times the *Metropolitan* had published the work of Theodore Dreiser and Joseph Hergesheimer, its most frequent contributor under Macfadden was his protégé, (Charles) Fulton Oursler, who tended to focus on the cheaply sensational himself.

Editor Hovey accepted four of the five stories Fitzgerald submitted to him through Ober over the next two years, declining only "The Curious Case of Benjamin Button." The first published, "The Jelly-Bean" in October 1920, is set in the same Tarleton, Georgia, that framed "The Ice Palace." The title character is one Jim Powell, a pool-playing, crap-shooting Southern idler who, one stimulating night, falls in love with town flapper Nancy Lamar. Overnight he resolves to make something of himself, only to find out the next morning that Nancy, intoxicated, has married an outsider she didn't really love. Jim quickly slips back into his jelly-bean ways. The story can be construed as less than happy—the reason Piper offers for its not having appeared in the *Post* (p. 68)—although others have noted that its plot and narrative structure echo "The Ice Palace." In fact, Ober apparently suggested that Fitzgerald give the story a happy ending, but he resisted, and the *Metropolitan* accepted it without hesitation.

Like "The Jelly-Bean," two of the three other stories Fitzgerald published in the *Metropolitan* have received some critical attention. "His Russet Witch" (February 1921)—later retitled "O Russet Witch!" when it appeared in *Tales of the Jazz Age*—is an almost surreal piece concerning one man's periodic encounters with a mysterious woman. His last meeting with her in old age confirms his suspicions that she is a romantic projection of his imagination, but in the scene immediately following he learns all the rational explanations of the mysteries he has witnessed. His life's sole bridge to the realm of romance has been burned. He "had wasted earth" by "resisting too many temptations."

Far different in tone and technique but somewhat similar in theme is "Winter Dreams," Fitzgerald's last short story in the *Metropolitan*, published in December 1922. Protagonist Dexter Green becomes enchanted with the lovely and desirable Judy Jones, and throughout his adolescence and young adulthood she becomes the symbol for everything romantic in his life and the inspiration for his success, a situation that foreshadows *The Great Gatsby*. When reality thuds home at the story's conclusion, and Dexter discovers Judy is unhappily married and losing her beauty, he mourns the passing of romance from his life. The story is considered one of the best of the author's early career.

Fitzgerald liked "The Jelly-Bean," "His Russet Witch," and "Winter Dreams" well enough to republish all three in hardcover, the first two in *Tales of the Jazz Age*, the last in *All the Sad Young Men*. As a group they represent the melancholy underside of Fitzgerald's romantic ethos. Though all these stories share the strong, desirable female and the desiring, potentially ambitious male of Fitzgerald's *Post* fiction, in the *Metropolitan* tales the romantic yearnings and ambitions are never satisfied—they are, in fact, dashed in a manner almost smartly cynical. None are as cynically romantic, however, as the author's *Smart Set* pieces.

In April 1922, a few months before the appearance of "Winter Dreams," *Metropolitan* published another Fitzgerald story that could well have turned up in *The Smart Set*. This was "Two for a Cent," a trivial tale that turns on an O. Henry-like twist of fate: the loss of a penny by one man, which ruins his life, and the discovery of the same penny by another, which starts him on the road to financial success. Fitzgerald himself acknowledged the story's lack of "vitality" (*Dear Scott*, p. 60); it could be best be compared with the earlier "The Smilers." *Metropolitan* also serialized *The Beautiful and Damned* in monthly installments from September 1921 through March of 1922, though in an edited version of its own that contemporary Thomas A. Boyd maintained "'was nothing but cheap sensationalism without any coherence at all'" (In *F. Scott Fitzgerald: In His Own Time*, Matthew J. Bruccoli, ed., New York: Popular Library, 1971, p. 250). Considering the magazine's weakness and the strength of Fitzgerald's popularity at this time, this editing of the novel was probably the only effect the periodical's editorial policies had on Fitzgerald's material published there. The author knew that what Carl Hovey refused could be sold elsewhere; he thus had considerable freedom to produce the sort of fiction with which he most desired to be identified.

Much of this fiction continued to show the influence of Mencken and Nathan. Fitzgerald had come to believe, with Mencken, that literary seriousness equalled a sort of naturalistic pessimism, a point of view reflected almost to a fault in *The Beautiful and Damned*. One somber tale that coincided with the beginning of his *Metropolitan* contract was "The Lees of Happiness," published in the 12 December 1920 fiction section of the *Chicago Sunday Tribune*. Yet another tale of romantic loss, in this case there is some indication that the loss strengthens the character of the losers—a man who has lost his wife to riches and a woman who has lost her husband to paralysis and death. Both develop the power to take the best from the past—"the lees of happiness"—and face the future alone, without even taking the obvious step of marrying each other. Considerably more frivolous—indeed, much in Fitzgerald's undergraduate vein—were two pieces written for *Vanity Fair*, a periodical that frequently published Nathan's work. "This is a Magazine" (December 1920) and "Jemina, the Mountain Girl" (January 1921) merit comparison with "Mr. Icky." Like it they are sophomoric, slapstick, and barely worth noting.

Two *Smart Set* pieces of this period—"Tarquin of Cheapside" and "The Far-Seeing Skeptics"—have already been mentioned. Near the end of his *Metropolitan* contract, he also published one story in *The Saturday Evening Post*, "The Popular Girl," which, at 15,000 words, was too long to be placed anywhere else. Even the *Post* broke it into two installments, not an unusual practice for the magazine, and it ran in the 11 and 18 February 1922 numbers. Ober had no trouble selling it; in fact, Lorimer was finding 1922 a skimpy year for fiction because so many writers were heading for Hollywood and "easy money" (Tebbel, p. 78). The 1922 *Post* had less than a hundred pages, half that of the *Post* of 1920, and few but Lorimer's regulars appeared there, for instance, Emerson Hough with "The Covered Wagon," Harry Leon Wilson with "Merton of the Movies," and newcomer John P. Marquand with "Only a Few of Us Left," a serial story about a dying family of aristocrats.

"The Popular Girl" features another ex-debutante-turned-husband-hunter named Yanci Bowman. Her plight grows desperate when her alcoholic father dies at the end of the first half, leaving her a fortune in debts. What follows is another of those elaborate schemes designed to attract a potential mate: Yanci collects her meager inheritance and literally goes for broke, intent on impressing wealthy prospect Scott Kimberly with her worldliness and popularity. No sooner has she spent her last dime and given up hope than Scott suddenly appears with the news that he has known of her situation for some time and wants to love and care for her for life.

Fitzgerald considered this story "precisely [*Post*] stuff" (*As Ever*, p. 29). He also referred to it more than once as "cheap." Shortly after selling it, he told Ober:

The Price of Paradise

> You notice that *The Popular Girl* hasn't the vitality of my earlier popular stories even tho I've learned my tricks better now and am technically proficient...in *The Popular Girl* I was merely repeating the *matter* of an earlier period without being able to capture the exuberant *manner*. (*As Ever*, p. 34)

In this instance, Fitzgerald's critical evaluation is pretty accurate. The overall motifs have changed little from his earliest *Post* stories, but there is no question this one is less lively. This problem arose here, as it would again later, because Fitzgerald had set out intentionally to write what he considered a *Post* story. By this point in his career, he had drawn a sharp line between the craft of writing for the popular press and the art of producing literature, and he had come to believe—with his intellectual contemporaries—that he could never publish literature in *The Saturday Evening Post*.

He was also experimenting with a new mode of short fiction that had so far been unsuccessful in the magazines, a fantasy mode represented in this period by "The Curious Case of Benjamin Button" and "The Diamond as Big as The Ritz." The first story, rejected by the *Metropolitan* as too outrageous, treats Fitzgerald's perennial theme of youth and age in an unusual fashion by featuring a man who is born a seventy-year-old and who then grows younger as time passes. In his prime, at the turn of the century, he fights as a young Army officer, and then becomes a college football hero. Yet, eventually, excessive youth has the same effect as excessive age, and as Benjamin shrinks back through the increasing helplessness of childhood toward embryonic sleep, the burlesque nature of the story makes way for the hauntingly poignant conclusion. It may well have ended up in *The Smart Set* too, had *Collier's* not snapped it up and published it in the 27 May 1922 number. Though yet another general interest periodical imitative of the *Post*, the 1922 *Collier's* was a mere thirty-five pages long, a victim of financial problems and frequent changes of editorial command. The magazine carried no more work by Fitzgerald in this phase of his career, and by itself exercised no influence over his work; it was simply a market of last resort, willing to take what Fitzgerald offered to trade on his name.

"The Diamond as Big as The Ritz" appeared in the June 1922 *Smart Set*, sent there as a personal favor to George Jean Nathan after it was rejected by the *Post*, *McCall's*, and *Harper's Bazaar*. "Diamond" is now one of Fitzgerald's best-known stories; it tells the strange, ironic tale of a young man who visits a school friend in the Far West, only to find his friend's father, Braddock Washington, is secretly the wealthiest man in the world, inheritor of a mountain-sized diamond. Most of the story plays with the idea of absolute wealth and the sensual and moral decadence it produces. It ends with the outside world's discovery and invasion of Washington's compound and an aerial battle during which Washington tries to bribe God. There was much here for *Smart Set* readers to enjoy: the decadent luxury, the exotic nature of the premise, the paradoxical inversion of American values, and assorted other ironies and blasphemies. Consciously and unconsciously, Fitzgerald still could not help associating literary worth with the principles of Mencken and, to a lesser extent, Nathan.

During the course of his *Metropolitan* contract, Fitzgerald also turned up often in print as a reviewer of novels by his contemporaries. In addition, he produced on request a handful of autobiographical notes and articles, such as "What I Think and Feel at Twenty-Five" (*The American Magazine*, September 1922), reflecting continued interest in the young author as a representative of his generation. At the end of 1922, when the *Metropolitan* finally succumbed to receivership, Ober arranged another agreement with the Hearst company that gave *Cosmopolitan* editor Ray Long first refusal on Fitzgerald's output for 1923 or a minimum of six stories. Four were ultimately accepted and two returned. The accepted stories ended up not in *Cosmopolitan*, however, but in its sister publication, *Hearst's International*.

Both Hearst periodicals were also imitating the successful *Post* format to some extent, and in fact had raided Lorimer's stables in 1922, carrying off authors like Ring Lardner, Irvin S. Cobb, and Clarence Budington Kelland. Ray Long, seeking big names at the time in a bid for increased circulation, was willing to pay Fitzgerald upwards of $1,750 per story. Fitzgerald had reservations about his ability to please at that price; he felt that Long "was not particularly sold on my stuff," and that Norman Hapgood, editor of *Hearst's International*, was "positively hostile." Indeed, he expressed to Ober his doubt that he was capable of turning out popular fiction at all (*As Ever*, p. 51). On the other hand, *Hearst's* had not lost touch with the more elevated literary tradition of previous decades under editors like William Dean Howells. Amid serials by popular suspense and romance writers E. Phillips Oppenheim, A. Conan Doyle, Edwin Balmer, and Kathleen Norris, one

The Price of Paradise

could also find work by H. G. Wells, W. Somerset Maugham, and William Rose Benét.

Apparently, both Fitzgerald and Hearst editors expected his fiction to be along popular lines. His first story in *Hearst's*, "Dice, Brass Knuckles, and Guitar," was published in May 1923 with the headline "A Typical Fitzgerald Story." It brings together the jellybean, the flapper, and the young aristocrats of the moneyed Northeast in an unlikely combination. Jim Powell of "The Jelly-Bean" goes north to open a jazz school for the idle young rich, where he teaches dancing, crapshooting, guitar, and self-defense, partly in an attempt at making money and partly to win his way into high society and the heart of a lovely young woman. In a climactic scene that reminds him of his "place," his school falls apart with his plans. He discovers, however, that the object of his affection, a high-class woman, has fomented—in the fashion of other Fitzgerald stories—an elaborate plot to win him. Too conscious of their differences, he turns his back on her and heads south again. Despite clear parallels with the other Tarleton-based stories, "The Ice Palace" and "The Jelly-Bean," this story is more clearly comic—so light, in fact, it barely holds together. It is significant at best only for making use of *Gatsby* motifs: the callousness of the rich and the pretentions of an outsider who tries to work his way in, unsuccessfully, for the sake of a woman.

A few months later, in August 1923, *Hearst's* published "Hot and Cold Blood," a genteel tale with an O. Henry twist. Here a young man learns, at his wife's urging, to be less generous and considerate. At the climax he refuses to give his seat on a streetcar to a standing woman; only when she faints beside him does he discover the woman is his pregnant wife. He ends up opting for his original warmth of spirit. A piece of popular morality, it shares little with his best work. Fitzgerald's next under this contract, "Diamond Dick and the First Law of Woman," published in April 1924, was another blatantly popular tale with, however, one *Gatsby* motif: the heroine, who calls herself Diamond Dick, strives to repeat a past romance. She succeeds, too; in an old-fashioned romantic twist, it turns out she had been married all along to her former lover, but that a war injury had made him forget that fact. She wins him back at gunpoint. Fitzgerald at least seemed aware of this story's technical flaws and was probably referring to them when he wrote Ober: "It doesn't seem good. I started with one mood and plot and finished with another and somewhere in between there is a joint that shows" (*As Ever*, p. 55).

His last story for *Hearst's International*, "The Baby Party," appeared in February 1925. Like "Hot and Cold Blood," it demonstrates a moral lesson, though in a much less wooden and stagey manner. It also possesses the artistic advantage—often a mark of merit in a Fitzgerald story—of focusing on a single episode, the baby party that leads via a childish misunderstanding to a punching match between two of the fathers. Little time elapses between their sheepish parting and the mutual moves toward reconciliation that end the narrative. Though the ending may be somewhat sentimental, it follows logically from what has come before. Thus, while Fitzgerald wrote the story in a popular vein, it does not lack aesthetic value. It is certainly the best story in the *Hearst's* group.

Two stories were also declined under this contract: "Rags Martin-Jones and the Pr-nce of W-les" and "'The Sensible Thing.'" It is somewhat difficult to understand why. The first story features an archetypal Fitzgerald flapper and overflows with whimsical "jazz" effects. Again we have the hero staging an elaborate deception to win the heroine, the wealthy, thrill-seeking Rags; here he fakes his own arrest in a rooftop speakeasy of his own invention in the presence of a party who is supposedly the Prince of Wales incognito. So taken is Miss Martin-Jones by this imaginative display, perpetrated by a man she believed had no imagination, that she capitulates in a fashion analogous to Ardita's in "The Offshore Pirate." This piece of fiction ended up in the July 1924 *McCall's* with the blurb, "The writer who discovered the flapper tells how one of them acts when she meets a real prince—in this, one of the best loved stories of the day."

"'The Sensible Thing'" was more sober than the other fiction Fitzgerald had offered, which may explain its rejection. It begins as a story of love frustrated by the hero's inability to make enough money to suit his beloved; the situation is lightened somewhat by his adolescent and misfiring attempt to change her mind. Following an interval of some years, an apparent romantic resolution arises with the return of the young man, bronzed and enriched by a sojourn in South America. After much further persuasion, the woman accepts his proposal, but with the realization on both their parts that in waiting this long, under the circumstances "the sensible thing" to do, they have lost the magic spontaneity of their earlier romance. A number of scholars have drawn attention to this piece for its *Gatsby* motif ("There are all kinds of love in this world, but never the same love twice"), and for the fictional parallels to Fitzgerald's own romance with Zelda. This story appeared in print in the 5 July 1924 issue of *Liberty*.

Both *McCall's*, a woman's magazine, and *Liberty*, a pale imitator of the *Post* more prone to the inspirational and sensational pieces Lorimer shunned, were eager to get work by Fitzgerald. He remained a popular figure in the print media four years after the splash of his initial success, still associated with youth, love, jazz, flappers, and "the modern point of view," and repeatedly named "spokesman of the New Generation" and "Chronicler of the Jazz Age." As such, he was yet as much in demand as a writer of articles as he was an author of short stories. Women's magazines in particular were interested in his views of marriage and child-rearing. In "Imagination—and a Few Mothers" (*Ladies' Home Journal*, June 1923), Fitzgerald mildly satirizes the old-fashioned "uplift" methods of child guidance and argues for permissiveness. In "'Wait Till You Have Children of Your Own!'" (*Woman's Home Companion*, July 1924), he speaks along similar lines, though with a more severe Menckenesque lambasting of the genteel generation of the nineties. His rhetoric is tempered at the conclusion, however, as he paints a sentimental picture of himself as an old man handing the world on to the next generation.

Fitzgerald expanded upon his views on marriage in a number of articles commissioned by various periodicals. The most significant of this period all appeared in 1924: "Does a Moment of Revolt Come Sometime to Every Married Man?" (*McCall's*, March), "'Why Blame It on the Poor Kiss if the Girl Veteran of Many Petting Parties Is Prone to Affairs After Marriage?'" (*New York American*, February 24), and "What Kind of Husbands Do 'Jimmies' Make?" (*Baltimore American*, March 30). As in his earlier articles, one finds in these, below the "modern" rhetoric, little that is inconsistent with middle-class values, particularly those of the middle class rising in the twenties. As one journalist, at the end of a typical interview with Fitzgerald, summed up the author's position, "Evidently the younger generation, whatever the vagaries of its head, still believes in keeping its heart in the same old place!" (Marguerite Mooers Marshall, "Our American Women Are Leeches," in *F. Scott Fitzgerald: In His Own Time*, p. 258).

Of the two most noteworthy publishing events of Fitzgerald's career that year, one was the June appearance of the short story "Absolution" in Mencken's new journalistic venture, *The American Mercury*. Considered one of Fitzgerald's best stories, "Absolution" is a subtle tale about a mad priest and the romantic, guilt-ridden farm boy whom he unintentionally liberates from Catholicism. It was excised from an early version of *The Great Gatsby* and shows the same artistic control of materials—the seriousness of purpose, the objective distance of the narrator, the irony and the careful understatement. Though undoubtedly *The American Mercury*, like *The Smart Set*, was a market of last resort because of its low pay rates, Fitzgerald was still much in awe of Mencken's critical powers and public influence and hoped to keep him on his side through the publication of *Gatsby*. Fortunately, "Absolution" fit well into the *Mercury* format, which was given to much nonfiction, and less fiction, on the theme of American life. Resolutely more serious than *The Smart Set*, a fact which led to Nathan's rapid departure, it featured tales full of local color and often critical of American values. Fitzgerald would only publish there once more, however, and would never write anything specifically for the magazine.

The other significant event of 1924 was Fitzgerald's reappearance as a regular writer for *The Saturday Evening Post*. He had avoided the magazine for much of his early career for fear of being regarded a *"Post* writer," which he believed, justifiably, would lower him in the eyes of most literary critics. Now, however, he needed the $2,000 per story Lorimer was willing to offer in the wake of the disasterous failure of his satirical play *The Vegetable*.

A glance at the 1924 *Post* shows that Lorimer's readership was concerned about immigration from Europe and financial aid *to* Europe and such domestic issues as the effect of credit buying. It was interested in the worlds of media and entertainment, radio, the Broadway stage, Hollywood, and figures of vaudeville and musical comedy. The fiction of 1924 reflected a number of these interests, with stories such as "Up from Heaven" by George Agnew Chamberlain, a tale of romance, success, and failure among stage people that ran in the March 15 issue. The same issue also contained more stories of reckless young aristocrats, on the whole more sympathetic than those of 1920, and others featuring the tough, two-fisted young man—soldier, sailor, farm boy, pioneer—a *Post* standard. And of course there were more business romances, in which young men of wit and grit win financially secure futures and usually a woman as well. The March 15 issue also carried the first story of this phase of Fitzgerald's *Post* career, "Gretchen's Forty Winks."

Fitzgerald's story itself carries some marks of the business romance, though not as many as would his next one, "The Third Casket." In "Gretchen's Forty Winks" the man on the move is Roger, a young

The Price of Paradise

advertiser-artist who must commit an unbroken six weeks to the account that will make his fortune. Meanwhile, the affections of his increasingly restless wife are being drawn away by the idle, quasi-aristocratic George. To hold his marriage together long enough to finish his work, he performs the morally questionable act of drugging his wife. Since in so doing he succeeds on all counts, however, the end again justifies the means, in the manner of business romances. Indeed, fate further blesses this course by visiting upon his rival George the very nervous breakdown George had predicted for him.

This staid, stylistically stripped story was followed on 31 May 1924 by "The Third Casket," a somewhat typical business romance in which an aging executive gives the three sons of three former associates the opportunity to prove themselves worthy of inheriting his business and his daughter. The winner is the one who seemed least likely to succeed: a Southerner who simply disappears after receiving his intructions. He returns just in time with an earned fortune and a *fait accompli* marriage with the daughter, thus demonstrating in daring but approved fashion his superior merit as a "go-getter." Like the previous story, it has the conservative air of having been written quickly to specifications.

Between these two stories, in the April 5 number, appeared Fitzgerald's essay "How to Live On $36,000 a Year." Its significance here lies largely in the manner Fitzgerald presented himself to *Post* readers. This Fitzgerald is no son of decayed aristocracy or smart young cynic, or even the wild young man of *Paradise* fame. He and his wife are instead "members of [the] newly rich class," distinctly bourgeois, basically naive (almost childishly so), and extravagant mainly because they are not accustomed to having money. Though the article may seem poignant today in view of what we know about Fitzgerald's perpetual financial troubles, the whole is cast in the mode of mildly ironic, masculine humor characteristic of the magazine—a comic edge further enhanced by cartoon-like illustrations. A follow-up article, "How to Live On Practically Nothing a Year," appeared a few months later in the 20 September 1924 number. It is less successful, its humor much more along sophomoric *Princeton Tiger* lines, giving way occasionally to brief passages of romantic description that look ahead to the European settings of many subsequent stories.

His other *Post* pieces of 1924 were "The Unspeakable Egg" and "John Jackson's Arcady." The first, published July 12, features yet another elaborate scheme, this time perpetrated by a wealthy young man who wishes to prove to his ex-fiancée that he is not "too perfect" for her. He does so by disguising himself as a churlish low-life and threatening her and her companions at a New England vacation cottage. When he finally reveals himself, it turns out his fiancée had known it was him for some time, and all ends happily. The story is melodramatic and improbable. "John Jackson's Arcady" appeared within the month in the July 26 issue. It has received a little critical notice because it treats a theme from *Gatsby*; John Jackson leaves his successful career and his unhappy homelife to return to the girl of his youth. She, in turn, resides in the small, midwestern town where they grew up, trapped in a loveless marriage with children. In a passionate moment she vows to run away with him, but later reverses herself and opts to remain with her family. Beaten, Jackson returns to the city. Logically, the story should have concluded here, but Fitzgerald added a happy ending in which Jackson is publicly cheered by the citizenry for his philanthropy, just before his prodigal son comes remorsefully home.

Over the next two years—1925 and 1926—Fitzgerald would place four more stories in the *Post*. He would also sell four to *Woman's Home Companion* (one would not appear until 1927) and three to *The Red Book*. Of this group the worst appeared in the *Woman's Home Companion*; Fitzgerald apparently thought little of that magazine as a market for his short fiction and allowed Ober to place there pieces the author could not or would not sell elsewhere. The first of these was "The Pusher-in-the-Face," which was published in February 1925, the month that "Baby Party," his last story under his *Hearst's* contract, saw print. It is an atypical Fitzgerald story about a limp little man who wins his revenge on the world by pushing people in the face. The story was atypical for the magazine as well, which generally featured stories of love, marriage, and family life and articles on the same. One could also find samples of the increasingly popular murder mystery and children's tales by writers like A. A. Milne.

Despite the appearance of *Post* writers like Ben Ames Williams in the *Companion* and even serious authors like Willa Cather, Fitzgerald continued to dump his worst material on the magazine. His "One of My Oldest Friends," published as the lead story of the September 1925 issue, is vaguely reminiscent of "Hot and Cold Blood," with a man turning away a friend in need at his wife's encouragement. He immediately repents, however, and chases his friend to a train station, where a telephone pole that takes the form of a crucifix directs the hero to the spot where his hapless associate is about to throw himself under a train.

Fitzgerald recognized that such baldly moralistic touches made the story inappropriate for the *Post*, and urged Ober not to offer it to Lorimer on the grounds that the ending was "a little sensational" (*As Ever*, p. 59).

The dubious best of the bad lot was "Not in the Guidebook," though Fitzgerald confessed at points in its composition and marketing that "it was rotten" (*As Ever*, p. 74) and "unsaleable in the big markets" (*As Ever*, p. 77). Published November 1925, it begins with a bad marriage between a second-generation American girl and a supposed war hero who is using shell shock as an excuse to remain drunk and idle. When the couple goes to Europe on her money to give him a new start, he deserts her. She ends up in the hands of a resourceful young American ex-soldier who runs a small touring operation. After they fall in love, it turns out, by an incredible coincidence, that he was the one who should have received the honors her husband won by theft. The light-hearted, first-person authorial voice that opened the narrative makes all well at the conclusion, assuring the reader of the new couple's happy marriage.

That the *Woman's Home Companion* must have been eager to accept anything from Fitzgerald provided it violated no taboos is evident from the last story of his it published. "Your Way and Mine" appeared well after the previous three stories in May 1927, just before Fitzgerald entered his most intense period of *Post* publication. It is a poorly constructed tale of a businessman of the nineties who does everything slowly and methodically until he finds himself passed up by his competitors. When he tries to do things their way, however, he ends up paralyzed from a nervous breakdown. Then the story suddenly jumps to the twenties, where the man has to choose between two suitors for his daughter: one efficient, one independent if stumbling. At the last minute, the man switches his preference to the latter, seeing in him shades of himself. Fitzgerald was correct when he wrote Ober, "This is one of the lowsiest [sic] stories I've ever written. Just terrible!" He goes on to say:

> Please—and I mean this—don't offer it to the *Post*. I think that as things are now it would be a *wretched* policy. Nor to the *Red Book*. It hasn't *one* redeeming *touch* of my usual spirit in it. I was desperate to begin a story + invented a business plot—the kind I can't handle. I'd rather have $1,000, for it from some

obscure place than have twice that + have it seen. *I feel very strongly about this*! (*As Ever*, p. 87)

Woman's Home Companion paid him $1,750 for this story, fair remuneration for a story he considered third-rate from a market he did not seriously cultivate.

If his worst fiction was heading for the *Companion*, his best, in his opinion, was going to *The Red Book Magazine*, which he considered "more hospitipal [sic] to my more serious work" (*As Ever*, p. 82). Over 1925-1926 *Red Book* printed three Fitzgerald stories, one of them widely judged to be among his best. At first glance, *The Red Book* looks like another *Post* imitator, with unfortunate leanings, like its competitors *Liberty* and *American*, toward the sensational and inspirational. The usual *Post*-style love stories, adventure tales, and humorous pieces—many by *Post* writers such as Struthers Burt and Hugh Wiley—are interspersed with a wide range of works one would not find in the *Post*. At the inspirational end are uplifting articles by figures like Bruce Barton, who produced the best-selling book, *The Man Nobody Knows*, that treated Jesus Christ, reverently, as a successful business manager. On the other end were daring pieces by the likes of Judge Ben B. Lindsey, a controversial individual known for his endorsement of the new sexual morality and open marriage and for his defiance of the Ku Klux Klan. In a similar vein was the fiction of Herbert Asbury, an author whose appearance in *The American Mercury* had led to Mencken's prosecution by the Boston Watch and Ward Society. The willingness of *The Red Book*'s editor to accept material that other general interest periodicals considered unwholesome or pessimistic gave the magazine a wider thematic range than most others and led Fitzgerald to contribute work to it he believed he could not sell elsewhere.

His first publication in *The Red Book*, pursuant to a 1924 request from its editor, was "The Adjuster," a story Fitzgerald called "a peach" (*As Ever*, p. 70), though "too gloomy" for most markets (*As Ever*, p. 73). Actually, it is also too mystical and pointedly moral for a magazine like the *Post*. Published in September 1925, it features a selfish ex-flapper who wishes to leave her home and family for the glitter and fun of the world outside. Her care-worn husband introduces her to a mysterious Doctor Smith (Doctor Moon in the version in his collection *All the Sad Young Men*) just before he, the husband, collapses with a mental breakdown. Much against her will, she is forced to preside over the care of her husband, the death of her child, and the operation of her household. No sooner has she finally accepted these responsibilities than the doctor disappears. Years later, we see her and her husband approaching middle age, caring for two children and contently enduring the redundant daily regimen of maintaining a home. Much like "The Lees of Happiness," this story combines a sort of melancholy with a firm message regarding moral strength and resignation in the face of adversity and the passage of time.

Fitzgerald's next story for *The Red Book* was "The Rich Boy," which appeared in two parts in the January and February issues of 1926. He had set out to write it specifically for the magazine, though he considered sending it to H. N. Swanson, editor of the new *College Humor* (and later Fitzgerald's Hollywood agent), who had been begging him for stories. Though he feared its realism would make it difficult to sell, *The Red Book* paid him $3,500 for it, the most he had received so far for a short story. This well-known and widely praised narrative concerns one Anson Hunter, who grows up a child of the very rich, with the power to do almost anything but satisfy his own desires. Fitzgerald uses one technique here that often marks one of his better stories, an observer-narrator who performs a minor role in the plot, permitting the author a great deal of commentary that in his own voice might seem intrusive. On the other hand, the story takes place over several years, a practice that often spells disaster in a Fitzgerald story; here it works, however, because the narrator does such an effective job of bridging the temporal gaps.

Through the narrator, we look on as Anson reaches young manhood, ruins a good match through drunkenness, inconsideration, and then stubborn hesitation, ends an affair with a debutante just short of consummation, blackmails his aunt into terminating an affair of her own, loses his friends to matrimony, then observes his original and only true love, Paula, in a scene of marital bliss with her second husband. The last vignette, of Anson on an ocean liner with the narrator, shows the protagonist somewhat callously recouping his good spirits after learning that Paula had died in childbirth. Fitzgerald overdoes nothing, avoiding melodrama and glossing even the more sensational moments, such as the aunt's lover's suicide, with ironic understatement. The story is a finely drawn portrait of character, without the elaborate plot or stagey devices that fill so much of his popular fiction. All it has in common with "The Adjuster" is its sobriety and the absence of standard romantic formulas.

Having found a market amenable to his serious work, Fitzgerald seemed uninterested in or incapable of sustaining the artistic standards of "The Rich Boy." He followed it up with one of the worst stories he ever wrote, "The Dance," which *The Red Book* published in June 1926. Like the business story, it belonged to another genre he could not work in, the murder mystery. The heroine is a New York flapper who is present at a small town dance where a man is shot to death. She eventually figures out the crime in a plot too thin even for good melodrama, having almost nothing in the way of suspense and action. Yet the magazine, which was accustomed to publishing much better mysteries by authors like Sir Arthur Conan Doyle and Arthur Somers Roche, took this one at a good price.

Fitzgerald's non-fiction output for 1925 and 1926 showed a sharp decrease from that of earlier years, at least in part because it was less lucrative than his fiction. Also, half a decade after his initial success, he was no longer the only spokesman youth had. His sole article in 1925 was one commisioned by *McCall's* and entitled "What Became of Our Flappers and Sheiks?" Here Fitzgerald humorously treats the evolution of the "sheik," while Zelda, in a parallel essay, discusses the flapper; the whole is accompanied by the comic illustrations of John Held, Jr. Fitzgerald's more earnest side manifested itself in his sole non-fiction piece of 1926, "How to Waste Material," his essay-review of Hemingway's *In Our Time* in the May *Bookman*. There were a couple of minor fictional pieces elsewhere, one of which—"Our Own Movie Queen" in the 7 June 1925 number of the *Chicago Sunday Tribune*—was largely the work of Zelda Fitzgerald.

Fitzgerald's *Post* stories of 1925 and 1926 continued in the mediocre vein of 1924. "Love in the Night" (14 March 1925) again uses the *Gatsby* motif of lost love, this time between a Russian prince disenfranchised by the Revolution and an adolescent woman mismatched in marriage to an older man. After one night of romance, they drop out of one another's lives for several years, only to re-encounter at the scene of their original tryst, where he now works as a menial and she, a wealthy widow, docks her yacht. Predictably, they live happily ever after. "A Penny Spent" (10 October 1925) is interesting only in that it takes the situation and setting of his essay of a year before—"How to Live On Practically Nothing a Year"—and turns it into fiction. In the story, the young man so talented at losing money saves the lives of the family of a wealthy American businessman by literally throwing money away when they are attacked by Italian highwaymen.

The twist on the business romance formula ends in the usual manner with the hero winning an executive position in the businessman's firm and his daughter's hand in marriage.

In "Presumption" (9 January 1926), the hero is a middle-class midwesterner bent on winning a daughter of northeastern aristocracy (*Gatsby* again?). After some initial failures based largely on class differences, he finds her engaged. This time persistence wins out; he alienates all parties from one another and at the last moment gains the woman's favor. "The Adolescent Marriage" (6 March 1926) begins with the separation of an immature husband and wife. The husband then submerges himself—*à la* "Gretchen's Forty Winks"—in his work and creates thereby a small architectural masterpiece, a house that embodies his lost love. As he moves into it, an older intermediary brings back his wife, who is pregnant. The sanctity of marriage is reaffirmed, and all will now presumably be well.

Of all these four, the one that probably comes closest to the stories by other authors appearing in the *Post* is "Love in the Night." An example would be Maude Parker Child's "Romance" (19 September 1925), in which a woman on the brink of middle age receives an invitation to an ambassadorial ball given by a European prince with whom she spent a romantic night two decades before. When her story-long reverie ends, she affirms her dull but satisfying marriage by turning down the invitation. The appearance of such motifs in and out of Fitzgerald's work suggests that fiction formulas are here in operation. If so, however, it must be recalled that these motifs—lost love and extramarital romance cut short by fidelity—also inform a masterpiece like *The Great Gatsby*, published in 1925. One can conclude that it is not the existence of formulas but Fitzgerald's handling of them in any one work that stands as a measure of his artistry. The themes of *Gatsby* appear in many short stories by Fitzgerald (and by others) in the *Post* and elsewhere, few of which even begin to demonstrate the skill shown in the novel.

Fitzgerald's magazine work from the end of 1920 through 1926 demonstrates a wide range of styles, story types, and aesthetic values. Thematically, at least half deal with young love or romanticism, and roughly half of these with romantic disillusionment (like "Winter Dreams"). A few conclude with moral lessons (for instance, "The Adjuster") and a few others feature successful romances, built around one partner's winning of the other (such as "Rags Martin-Jones and the Prnce of W-les"). The many non-romances are scattered through categories of moral instruction, parody, fantasy, Menckenesque irony, and a tiny sampling of others. In tone, the above pieces swing from the serious, realistic, and artistically admirable "The Rich Boy" to the weak, silly, and poorly composed "The Third Casket" and "The Pusher-in-the-Face," from the moralistic "Hot and Cold Blood" to the wildly cynical "The Diamond as Big as The Ritz." With the possible exception of the *Post* stories, few of these, however, were written with specific markets in mind; by and large Fitzgerald was writing what he wanted to write or what he thought would sell, while leaving Ober the task of finding a suitable buyer. These stories thus reflect less the imposition of particular editorial guidelines than Fitzgerald's perceptions of his audience as a whole, if not his own artistic preferences.

One can infer much about these perceptions and preferences from the stories he chose to include in the last short story volume to come out of this period, the 1926 *All the Sad Young Men*, for which Fitzgerald skimmed off what he considered the cream of his 1922-1926 output. Out of the nine pieces in his original scheme for the book, only one had been published in the *Post* ("Gretchen's Forty Winks"); the others were drawn from markets as far apart as *The American Mercury* and *McCall's*. Four are serious tales of some merit ("The Rich Boy," "Absolution," "Winter Dreams," "'The Sensible Thing'"), two are moral tales of rather genteel import ("The Baby Party," "Hot and Cold Blood"), and three are comedies ("Rags Martin-Jones and the Pr-nce of W-les," "Dice, Brass Knuckles and Guitar," "Gretchen's Forty Winks"). Before publication, Fitzgerald substituted "The Adjuster" for "Dice, Brass Knuckles and Guitar," dropping a jazz comedy in favor of a moral tale. The volume is thus heavily weighted toward the serious, with at least three of the stories at that end of the spectrum considered among the author's best. The reader who wanted straightforward moral lessons, however, or pure, frothy entertainment could find it in the book as well. "Once more," Robert Sklar notes, "Fitzgerald was all things to all people, as he had been when *This Side of Paradise* started his career so successfully" (p. 215).

Contemporary reviewers made mention of the variety of *All the Sad Young Men* as well. The kindest among them found in this fact "excellent proof of his ability to write well in half a dozen manners." The same reviewer went on to observe,

> It is a joy to read these tales. They lack sameness; they are ironical, and sad, and jolly good fun by

turns; they scintillate. Moreover, they show F. Scott Fitzgerald keeping step with his generation. He is of our own time and we are glad that he is. (Harry Hansen, "*All the Sad Young Men*: The Boy Grows Older," in *F. Scott Fitzgerald: In His Own Time*, p. 368)

Others less enthusiastic and less kind, such as William Rose Benét, sensed, not inaccurately, that "behind most of the writing in this book [lies] the pressure of living conditions rather than the demands of the spirit" ("*All the Sad Young Men*: Art's Bread and Butter," in *F. Scott Fitzgerald: In his Own Time*, p. 368). If Fitzgerald was torn between his status as an artist and his role as popular entertainer, it is clear that the majority of his critics—and no doubt his readers—continued to see him in 1926 as the spokesman of his generation and the writer of generally well-crafted, amusing, but often lightweight stories. Even the nature of what praise he received for *All the Sad Young Men* was damning to the serious article in him.

Ironically, Fitzgerald the serious artist could not make a living. By the end of 1926 he had received virtually all the money he would earn from *The Great Gatsby*, published only the year before to mixed reviews. Struggling to keep up with his still lavish lifestyle and perpetual debts, he tried once more to break into Hollywood as a screenwriter. While Ober attempted to negotiate a contract for him with *Liberty*, he commenced work on his next novel. When the *Liberty* contract—which would have paid him $3,500 per story—fell through, Fitzgerald turned again to Lorimer's *Post*. Thus, in 1927, began Fitzgerald's most intense period of writing for that magazine, a period during which he would publish almost nothing but *Post* fiction. It is probably, critically speaking, the most controversial phase of his career.

The Price of Paradise

III.
HITCHED TO THE *POST*

In July 1927 Fitzgerald received this message from his agency: "We have sold your story entitled JACOB'S LADDER to the Post for Three Thousand Dollars ($3,000.00). They say they like the story tremendously and are going to be very much disappointed if you don't do a lot more for them just as good" (*As Ever*, p. 98). The $3,000 figure was a significant jump over the $2,500 Fitzgerald had received for his last few *Post* stories. "Jacob's Ladder" may well also have been the first Fitzgerald story purchased by Lorimer's new associate editor Thomas B. Costain, with whom Ober would be dealing for the next several years. But most significant from the standpoint of Fitzgerald's career is that "Jacob's Ladder" was the first story Fitzgerald sold to this magazine, or even attempted to sell, that had an unhappy ending. Up to now Fitzgerald had believed that he could not sell his more "serious" work to the *Post*, which had led to his forcing happy endings onto such tales as "John Jackson's Arcady" (see above).

Briefly, "Jacob's Ladder" concerns one Jacob Booth, a wealthy New Yorker who encounters the lower-class teenager Jenny Delahanty at a trial, takes her under his protection, and helps her into the movies. While she is on her way to stardom as Jenny Prince, he falls in love with her. His opportunity to make her his has passed, however. Jacob visits her in Hollywood, where in a short melodramatic episode he saves her from blackmail, but he can elicit no proclamation of affection from her stronger than friendship. Ultimately, she accepts a marriage proposal from a director. His romantic hopes dashed, Jacob enters a Broadway movie house to watch onscreen the woman he helped create.

The critic John Higgins maintains that this story represents not only a substantial step upward in Fitzgerald's magazine career but a substantial change in editorial policy for the *Post*:

Even more important is the *Post*'s acceptance for the first time of a Fitzgerald story with a less-than-happy ending. A good number of his *Post* stories from this time until George Lorimer's departure from the *Post*'s editorship in 1932 have unhappy or only partially happy conclusions. This in part accounts for their superiority to many of their earlier stories that collapsed when a happy ending was forced upon them. There is no known declaration of a policy shift, yet there must have been one, for the *Post* had not accepted his earlier stories without happy endings. (p. 98)

He goes on to attribute this change to "an increase in Fitzgerald's popularity following *The Great Gatsby* and *All the Sad Young Men*" (p. 98).

If one looks only at Fitzgerald's stories in the *Post*, one might be led to believe, with Higgins, that the magazine had changed its policy regarding unhappy endings. Since this point touches crucially upon the question of Fitzgerald's "writing down" to fit *Post* parameters, it merits further discussion here. In actuality, if one reads widely in *The Saturday Evening Post* of the 1920s, one finds that stories with unhappy or only partially happy endings, while clearly in the tiny minority, had been appearing periodically since the beginning of the decade. Amid the love stories and business romances, the westerns, mysteries, adventure stories, and comic tales, the reader comes upon a story like Oscar Graeve's "The Poor Fish" (21 February 1920), in which an earnest if bumbling businessman courts his officious secretary to avoid losing a good employee to marriage to another man, only to fall in love with her himself. Then, thinking he is talking her out of marrying her betrothed, he inadvertently loses her.

A more striking example, especially in connection with "Jacob's Ladder," is the story that opened the 15 March 1924 issue in which "Gretchen's Forty Winks" appeared, George Agnew Chamberlain's "Up from Heaven." This tale opens with two Nathanesque, wealthy Broadway types, Trumper and Magyar, who pick up a low-class teenaged female on a Manhattan street. Trumper takes a particular interest in the girl, despite her brash language and manners, and attempts to win her by way of an elaborate scheme that falls through because of Magyar's intervention. As his interest in her grows, Trumper takes it upon himself to make her a star on Broadway. He accomplishes the feat, in the process falling in love with her, but he loses his creation to the fast-moving Magyar. In a poignant final scene, Trumper calls his ex-wife on the phone in the middle of the night, but she is too sleepy to talk to him.

The unhappy endings aside, a number of obvious parallels exist between "Jacob's Ladder" and "Up from Heaven." In both, the protagonist, a well-to-do, somewhat cynical New Yorker, discovers a very young, attractive woman, ill-bred and slangy, but with potential the protagonist soon recognizes. In both, the protagonist uses his power to get the woman started in the entertainment industry, after which her potential carries her to stardom. In each case, as she succeeds the man's love for her grows; in each, the man loses her to another. Both stories end with a sad scene emphasizing, with a touch of irony, the protagonist's defeat and isolation. Even the titles bear some similarity; both refer in some way to celestial ascent.

Concerning the inspiration for Fitzgerald's story, Robert Sklar maintains that it came out of his recent Hollywood infatuation with the young actress Lois Moran, model for Rosemary Hoyt of *Tender Is the Night* (p. 228). No doubt, considering the extent to which Fitzgerald used personal experience in his fiction, this romance may have served as partial inspiration, yet is at least a remarkable coincidence that a nearly identical situation forms the core of Chamberlain's story of three years previous. Another possibilty arises from Andrew Turnbull's contention that Fitzgerald kept in his notebooks outlines of *Post* stories by other writers (*Scott Fitzgerald*, New York: Scribner's, 1962, p. 287). It is almost certain that Fitzgerald came across "Up from Heaven," since it appeared immediately before "Gretchen's Forty Winks" in that issue. Chamberlain's theme of love lost must have appealed to the author who was working on *The Great Gatsby* at the time. Though one need not suggest that Fitzgerald consciously utilized specific materials of other *Post* writers, such practices were evidently not uncommon among Lorimer's regulars and those who wished to join them; as already noted, similar themes and plots recur frequently in the *Post*, as they do in all popular literature.

While lamenting that Fitzgerald so often "wrote down" to *Post* standards, most critics have failed to note that many of the magazine's so-called formulas left him plenty of aesthetic leeway. Higgins reiterates throughout his study that Fitzgerald worked out the motifs of his novels in his short stories, as demonstrated above by the repeated re-workings of *Gatsby* in numerous pieces. Furthermore, despite Higgins's observations and those of other scholars endorsing the accepted critical stance, nothing in Lorimer's editorial policy prevented Fitzgerald from publishing stories with less-than-happy endings before 1927. Having waited as long as he did to break out of the romantic comedy mode that he had identified with in the *Post*, he could not have done so more safely than with a tale of ironic pathos resembling closely one that had already been published, whether he did so intentionally or not.

In the next story for the magazine, Fitzgerald apparently attempted to do as requested by giving the editors more of the same. In "The Love Boat," published 8 October 1927, three wealthy college men board a yacht where a high school prom is ongoing. One of the men, Bill, falls in love with a charming, working-class girl named Mae, who is all but engaged to a boy of equivalent status. Years later, past his prime and unhappily married, Bill encounters Mae again and finds her content in wedlock with her former boyfriend. Trying to recapture the past, he crashes another high school prom on another yacht and there unsuccessfully courts a girl named May. After making a fool of himself, he returns home to find his wife gone, probably for good. Realizing his life has permanently altered for the worse, he stares out the window at "the bright uncapturable moon," symbol of "all the restless longing after fleeing youth in all the world."

This story shares a number of motifs with the previous one: the wealthy man's falling in love with a working-class girl, his losing her in marriage to another, and a small measure of ironic distance from the protagonist that changes to sympathy in a touching final scene. It also copies motifs from the earlier "Love in the Night" and "John Jackson's Arcady," particularly the Gatsby-like attempt to recapture one's youth by trying to rekindle love in a setting from the past. Indeed, "The Love Boat" has the conclusion that "Arcady" should have had, and might have if Fitzgerald had allowed himself unhappy endings in his *Post* stories of 1924.

Fitzgerald pulls away, albeit temporarily, from the lost love/love youth theme to return to the college settings of his youth for his next two stories. "A Short Trip Home" begins as a realistic tale of college types, but turns sinister with the appearance of a diabolic figure that haunts a young woman riding home from a prom weekend. The young hero, realizing that something is wrong, intervenes and saves the woman from what turns out to be the ghost of a hoodlum. This was one of Fitzgerald's few stories of the supernatural and his only one for the *Post*. As the editors indicated in their acceptance letter, the magazine rarely handled such things (*As Ever*, p. 103); Fitzgerald was so welcome in the magazine at this time, however, that not only was the story purchased, it was the featured piece of fiction in the 17 December 1927 issue.

"The Bowl" (21 January 1928) focuses on a number of college types even more recognizable to readers accustomed to football and other sports heroes in their fiction and non-fiction. The star in this case is reluctant quarterback Dolly Harlan, who gives up the game at the request of vamp Vienna Thorne, only to reject her in favor of saving his team during the big game. His opting for manhood, loyalty, and sacrifice is rewarded in conventional *Post* fashion by his winning not only the game, but also a better woman. If Fitzgerald was maneuvering outside of established *Post* genres in "A Short Trip Home," he was certainly giving the editors what they wanted in this story, consciously or unconsciously. "The Bowl" fits perfectly into the ubiquitous category of stories about tough young men, which was second only to the business romance as a staple of *Post* fiction.

Fitzgerald touched on another popular genre in his next piece for the magazine: the Hollywood story. "Magnetism," published 3 March 1928, tells the tale of George Hannaford, an actor so charismatic that women incessantly fall in love with him. In this story it is the teenaged actress that pursues the older man, reversing the motif of other stories, and almost destroys his happy marriage. Non-violent crime motivates the plot, as it does in much *Post* fiction, but with a bit of mild irony the readers would appreciate; the very charm that causes the blackmailing of Hannaford also ends it. Despite these conventional touches, some critics maintain that this is among Fitzgerald's better short stories, perhaps even the best to appear between "The Rich Boy" and the Basil stories (Higgins, p. 101). Like "The Bowl," however, it is fairly representative of mainstream *Post* fiction.

At this point in 1928, stories featuring strong female characters, an early specialty of Fitzgerald's, were enjoying a resurgence in the magazine. Most notable were Joseph Hergesheimer's "Coral," a series of stories about a willful though snobbish young heroine who pursues one man after another, only to reject each as not good enough, and Elizabeth Alexander's serial "Second Choice," about a vampish young lady too familiar with the ways of men. Masculine tales of action and adventure continued to be strongly represented in western stories and serials by Hal G. Evarts, Struthers Burt, and others, and sea stories, often set in the distant past, like those of F. Britten Austin. Also in a masculine vein were vernacular comedies by Clarence Budington Kelland, Octavus Roy Cohen, and Hugh Wiley. E. Phillips Oppenheim reappeared in the 1928 *Post* with another of his series on the theme of international suspense, this one called "The Human Chase." And Booth Tarkington returned to the *Post* stable with several stories featuring innocent young men up against a sophisticated world, while contributing a series of articles concerning the effects of urbanization on small-town life.

It may have been Tarkington's widening presence in the periodical's pages that inspired Fitzgerald to take his next course. The 28 April 1928 number of the *Post* contained "The Scandal Detectives," the first story of his first serial for the magazine, the Basil Duke Lee stories. More than one critic has expressed surprise that Fitzgerald should have returned at this stage to pre-*Paradise* autobiographical material for his fiction (see, for instance, Sklar, p. 232-33). Sklar suggests that the author may have been running short of subjects and thus turned back to the relatively unmined period of his early adolescence (p. 231). It is also Sklar who observes that the Basil stories reaffirm Fitzgerald's link with Tarkington; indeed, these stories owe as much to Tarkington as they do to Fitzgerald's boyhood: "Fitzgerald cut the stories straight from the Tarkington mold" (p. 232-33). The biggest difference from the older writer appears in Fitzgerald's handling of adolescent sexuality, a topic Tarkington chose to ignore in most of his fiction. Fitzgerald took up the challenge in eight stories that comprised most of his output for 1928.

The first two Basil stories are comedies. In "The Scandal Detectives," the fourteen-year-old hero plots an attack on rival Hubert Blair, only to provide the latter inadvertently with an edge in the winning of the disputed girl. In "A Night at the Fair" (21 July 1928) Basil overcomes setback after setback with fortune's help, only to find himself outdistanced by Hubert Blair once again. With "The Freshest Boy" (28 July 1928) the series takes a serious turn. Here Basil finds himself ostracized at prep school for being a conceited loudmouth. Like the earlier stories, this one climaxes at a moment of insight *cum* growth for Basil; in addition, he finally becomes "wise to himself," learning the value of humility, self-control, hard work, and cooperation. Through these newly won virtues he gains the longed-for acceptance from his peers and, symbolic of this, a nickname. The author gently hammers

The Price of Paradise

home, in a moralistic passage at the conclusion, the importance of Basil's lesson.

The lesson appears to have been forgotten by both protagonist and author, however, in the next story, another comedy. In "He Thinks He's Wonderful" (29 September 1928) Basil allows his apparent charm to go to his head, inducing him to unintentionally talk himself out of a vacation with the family of his favorite girl Minnie Bibble. He does receive a last minute consolation in being permitted to drive another girl around in his grandfather's automobile. Success is unquestionably his, finally, in "The Captured Shadow" (29 December 1928), though not, significantly, without some moral compromise. Basil writes and puts on a play that goes over extremely well in his community; however, in order to keep his leading lady from leaving town on a trip with her family, he purposely exposes her younger brother to the mumps. Amid the acclaim in which he basks at the story's end, this small sin still bothers him.

The efficacy of sin is further demonstrated in "The Perfect Life" (5 January 1929). Following a show of outstanding prowess during a football game, Basil is approached by an alumnus who persuades him to set an example of wholesome, genteel, moral living for others. But in trying to reform a flapperish young woman, he nearly drives her into an impulsive elopement with a ne'er-do-well. Basil manages to reverse the harm only by abandoning "the perfect life" and getting drunk with the wastrel to stop the elopement. The question of "greatness" vs. "goodness" that had come up in Fitzgerald's fiction since *This Side of Paradise* here reaches an unstable resolution in a manner that plays with gentle irony off of genteel expectations: it is "virtue" that causes harm, "vice" that corrects the situation. *Post* readers would have appreciated this droll irony and would have found familiar and acceptable the basic "end justifies the means" pragmatism of Basil's actions, common to many business stories and trickster comedies in the magazine's pages. Though Basil functions, Sklar emphasizes, as a conventional genteel-romantic boy hero in a line that extends back through Tarkington to Tom Sawyer, he shares with the less genteel Huck Finn the willingness to "go to hell" for what he believes to be right.

Fitzgerald invites further comparisons with the genteel boy hero in the last two Basil stories. "Forging Ahead" (30 March 1929)—the title was borrowed from a Horatio Alger novel—pits Basil's love of love against his desire for success. Forced to choose between escorting an undesirable girl as a condition of his job and dating the attractive Minnie Bibble, Basil is saved at the last moment by a *deus ex machina* in the form of sudden family wealth. In "Basil and Cleopatra" (27 April 1929), the last story published in the series, Basil liberates himself from Minnie's spell in the wake of further athletic triumphs, thereby winning the independence of spirit that will permit him to tread the path of "ambition, struggle, and glory." In other words, he has traded the romance of love for the romance of success.

Scholars disagree sharply on the merit of the Basil series, even of individual stories. Some find them technically deft, while others consider them artificial and unconvincing. Fitzgerald himself maintained that the "Basil Duke Lee stories were a mistake—it was too much good material being shoved into a lousy form," though adding "I thought they were better than the response they had" (*Letters*, p. 495). Nevertheless, he refused, despite the urging of Ober and Perkins, to bring the series together into a single volume, believing that doing so would hurt his reputation as a serious writer. He himself acknowledged that the stories were "full of Tarkington" (*Dear Scott*, p. 199).

Besides Tarkington and Fitzgerald, another *Post* regular could be found exploiting the *bildungsgeschichte* sub-genre in these issues. Before the Basil series ended, J. P. Marquand's "Warning Hill" had commenced (the first installment opened the issue that contained "Forging Ahead"). Marquand's serial concerns the maturation of a boy in a New England town up through his involvement in World War I, with particular emphasis on the interrelationship of his destiny with the women in his life, one rich, one a member of his own class. Marquand, probably the *Post* author most amenable to trends within the magazine and suggestions from Lorimer, also published another World War I story in "Oh, Major, Major," published in the number that also carried "Basil and Cleopatra." It concerns the wartime hostilities between a pompous officer and a no-nonsense non-com, hostilities that evaporate when the two men encounter years later.

Fitzgerald made his own contribution to wartime nostalgia with a period piece that appeared just before the end of the Basil series, his well-known "The Last of the Belles." Tucked away on page 18 of the 2 March 1929 number, it opens with an illustration of a brawny soldier standing over a frail-looking woman, aligning the story with the school of tough young men. In fact, however, the story shares with many of the stories of 1927-1929 the motif of loss—the loss of youth and romance. It also brings back the strong-willed, free-spirited young

The Price of Paradise

woman as central character and the first-person observer-narrator, both last seen in "The Bowl." Andy, a young enlistee, narrates the tale of his relationship with the coquettish Ailie Calhoun while at a southern training camp. Though unsuccessful as her lover, he becomes her confidante and watches her run through a number of other men, including a boob-like northern streetcar operator stationed at the camp; she eventually marries someone else. The story ends on a scene set several years later, with Andy stumbling through the ruins of the abandoned camp, "looking for my youth in a clapboard or a strip of roofing or a rusty tomato can."

The theme of aging and romantic disillusionment turns up once more in this phase of Fitzgerald's *Post* career, in the story "At Your Age," published 17 August 1929. Here the hero is nearly fifty, seeking the romance of youth in vain until he meets a society girl who falls in love with him. Following their engagement, however, he finds her wild ways disconcerting and in a climactic scene takes her mother's side against her. He loses the girl and thus "the battle against youth and spring," but contents himself with the lukewarm consolation of remembering their year-long affair. This story has more in common with the average *Smart Set* story of 1920 than the average *Post* story of 1929; nevertheless, it was the first piece of fiction in its issue, a placement that connotes editorial approval.

Only Lorimer's favorite writers could curry such high favor with such melancholy tales. Another was Sophie Kerr, whose "Yes, Sir; Thank You, Sir," published 5 January 1929, brings back the central motif of "Up from Heaven" and Jacob's Ladder": the older man who helps a working-class girl onto the stage, only to lose her. Yet another was Don Marquis; his "Exit the King," also published January 5, features a dying actor mulling over the disappointments and disillusionments of his life, particularly the women who destroyed him in his prime. The only thing of value he now possesses is an artifact of his youth, a letter of praise from Edwin Booth. He has enjoyed, like the hero of "At Your Age" a few months later, the faint glimmer of consolation a single memory can provide. Lost love and lost youth were not uncommon in the *Post* of the late twenties.

The strong, independent female protagonist also continued her dominance through 1929. Fitzgerald dipped back into this genre not only with the serious "The Last of the Belles," but also in the lighter "Majesty," which appeared 13 July 1929. Like many of Fitzgerald's weakest stories, this one jumps over great gaps of time and space, with little but authorial intrusions bridging the gaps. The flapperish heroine leaves her high-society groom to her staid cousin Olive, and the latter two look on as she turns up some years later in Europe with a suspicious character who claims to be royalty, then ends up as the minor monarch's wife attending a reception at Buckingham Palace. "Majesty" is definitely mediocre fiction, though Ober found it "beautifully written" and maintained that Costain thought it "splendid" (*As Ever*, p. 134), while Perkins wanted it included in *Taps at Reveille*, Fitzgerald's 1935 short story collection. Lorimer must have agreed with these assessments, because with the acceptance of this story and the very different "At Your Age" Fitzgerald's price rose to $4,000 per story.

Fitzgerald's two remaining stories of 1929 were "The Rough Crossing" and "The Swimmers," both serious tales concerning marital discord and having uncomfortably happy endings. The first was published in the June 8 number with illustrations giving the impression that it was a sea adventure story. The first two paragraphs set the atmosphere with a gloomy, foreboding description that Fitzgerald used almost verbatim in *Tender Is the Night*. This passage is not all the story shares with that novel, either; besides the strained marriage, one finds as well the motifs of the older man infatuated with the younger woman, a suggestion of insanity in the wife, and the background presence of Europe. Similar motifs appear in "The Swimmers," published a few months later in the October 19 issue of the *Post*. In "The Rough Crossing," the marital difficulties reach an uneasy resolution in a melodramatic climax in which Adrian Smith rescues his wife Eve from an apparent suicide attempt, followed by a quiet disembarkment in a European harbor where the Smiths deny they were themselves during the voyage. If the reader can deny the reality of the underlying Smiths, as Fitzgerald knowing his audience no doubt intended, then the story has reached a happy conclusion: all's well that ends well.

"The Swimmers" caused the *Post* more difficulty, since it hinges on the efforts of one Henry Marston to get free of his adulterous French wife without losing his two sons to her; Ober, in his letter notifying Fitzgerald of the story's acceptance, referred to "the part about the divorce, etc.," but added that the editors thought it "so unusually good that they could not resist it" (*As Ever*, p. 144). Perhaps one of the elements that redeemed the story is the ultimate success of the hero, won through cleverness, persistence, physical and moral strength, and the willingness to manipulate people and situations to his advantage—in short, all the characteristics of the business romance hero. We watch

The Price of Paradise

Marston recuperate from a nervous breakdown, caused by his wife's infidelity, and take up swimming under the tutelage of a wholesome American girl. When he ends up trapped on a small boat with his French wife and her semi-American lover Wiese—a boat that appears to be floating out to sea—he offers to swim to shore for help provided they sign his children over to him. Marston wins, although he knew all along the boat was actually floating to a safe haven. The Americanism of his virtues is underlined in an oft-quoted passage at the story's end, where the author refers to America as "a willingness of the heart." This patriotic finish could have overshadowed a good deal of suspect morality.

In the thirty-eight months between "Jacob's Ladder" and "The Swimmers," Fitzgerald published only one piece of fiction outside of the *Post*, the slight but artistically polished "Outside the Cabinet-Maker's" in the December 1928 issue of *The Century Magazine*. He also produced a small handful of vignettes for the *New Yorker*, *College Humor*, and some Princeton publications, none of the pieces significant. A few short stories appeared under his name and Zelda's in *College Humor*, though these were her work. As 1929 drew to a close, there could be no doubt that Fitzgerald was, for the time, a *Post* writer. He shared the magazine's pages predominately with other regulars: Harry Leon Wilson, E. Phillips Oppenheim, F. Britten Austin, J. P. Marquand, Booth Tarkington, and Bernard De Voto.

In the non-fiction department, perennial essayists Albert W. Atwood, Garet Garrett, Will Payne, and Edwin LeFevre followed the ups and downs of the stock market and its effect on mass production and mass consumption. For most of 1929 they viewed the American economy in terms that ranged from cautious optimism to boastful praise, but not surprisingly all that changed abruptly with the coming of the Crash. After a brief, stunned silence, the same writers began trying to analyze and explain what had happened; by the first issue (January 4) of 1930, LeFevre appeared on page 6 with "The Little Fellow on Wall Street," an evaluation of what the average citizen-investor had lost the previous October.

Fiction writers were one step behind with pieces like "Bull Market" by Julian Street, which opened the 18 January 1930 number. Beginning in the boom year of 1928, its first paragraphs are full of then obvious ironies about stock fortunes and the market remaining bull forever. The rest of the story catalogues the evils of quick riches. We first see the protagonist hung over after a wild party, talking his butler into investing his life savings in the market. Then we watch as wealth from stocks destroys the protagonist's family: his son is crippled when his private plane crashes, his daughter elopes with his chauffeur—also enriched by the market—and his wife is considering an affair with her expensive interior decorator. By the time the market crashes, wiping out him and his butler, his family has disintegrated. The man ends up disappearing out his penthouse window.

Current events had thus introduced a new theme to the *Post*. While there had always existed those characters who misused riches, particularly if inherited, wealth alone, especially if earned through the American system of enterprise, had not been regarded as wicked and destructive *per se* until now. The *Post*, by way of the standards it set throughout the twenties in fiction, articles, and above all advertising, had encouraged Americans to become part of the party of the Boom even as it continued to laud such old American values as thrift and personal accountability. Now Lorimer and company felt perfectly justified in placing the suddenly irresponsible stock speculator in opposition to the hard-working saver, depicted in a 1 February 1930 editorial cartoon as respectively grasshopper and ant. Like the American middle class that made up the body of its readership, however, the *Post* could not leap so suddenly from the boom bandwagon without carrying an armload of residual guilt. In throwing the protagonist of "Bull Market" out the window, the author, editors, and readers were participating in the man's tragedy even as they remained ostensibly aloof from his obvious failures as a human being; they were killing a scapegoat as propitiation for their sins.

Though the onset of the Great Depression would not appear overtly in Fitzgerald's *Post* fiction for a few months yet, the theme of guilt and retribution suddenly and almost coincidentally looms very large in his 1930 stories. His first story of the year, "Two Wrongs," published in the January 18 issue that carried "Bull Market," reflects this new thematic emphasis. Protagonist Bill McChesney begins as a brash, successful young stage producer, but following a trend that will repeat itself often in Fitzgerald fiction of the thirties—most notably *Tender Is the Night*—he succumbs to his own darker tendencies towards drunkenness and violence. The moment of his lowest humiliation, getting thrown drunk from a party while attempting to flirt with titled ladies, coincides with his neglected wife's giving birth to a stillborn child. His debauchery eventually leads to tuberculosis, which forces him to head west alone, leaving his wife to pursue a dancing career that

The Price of Paradise

will take her away from him; in this way he atones for his sins. Though many critics see the inevitable connections in this story with Fitzgerald's own bouts with alcoholism, such personal suffering and remorse resonated through the pages of the magazine in this period. The national hangover had begun.

Still, the periodical preserved its preference for lighter fiction in the traditional optimistic manner: adventure stories, mystery series and serials (notably Earl Derr Bigger's Charlie Chan), mild satires by the likes of Tarkington and De Voto, college stories by Percy Marks, and many stories of tough young men—boxers, soldiers, sailors—who in the wake of the Crash seemed to have replaced the young businessman as the ideal American male. Despite the darkening economic picture, perhaps even because of it, the old rich, the aristocracy, was featured in a number of stories by regulars like Hergesheimer and Marquand. There was also, inevitably perhaps, a good deal of nostalgia, with stories set in the nineteenth century or around World War I. One of the latter was William Faulkner's first *Post* publication, "Thrift," which appeared 6 September 1930 alongside Mussolini's "My War Diary." Faulkner's story concerns a parsimonious Scotsman in the R.A.F. who inadvertently performs heroic deeds and turns down a series of honors, all for the sake of amassing as much money as possible before he returns to his highland farm.

Fitzgerald managed to combine a number of his favorite and most popular motifs in the series he began that year, his second and last series in the *Post*, the Josephine stories. Like the Basil series, this one returns to the prewar era, this time to trace the maturation of his earliest popular type, the flapper. In the process, the stories exploit the contemporary interest in nostalgia, the rich, college settings, and guilt and remorse. When we first meet her, Josephine Perry is a temperamental, impulsive, sexually aware girl of sixteen. Like the archetypal flapper of "The Offshore Pirate," she swears, tells her wealthy parents to "shut up," and does pretty much as she pleases, particularly in regard to men. "First Blood" (5 April 1930) introduces two motifs that will dominate the Josephine series, the ironic contrast between reputation and actual behavior and the overspending of emotional resources, which will end in "emotional bankruptcy." In this story, Josephine steals her older sister's boyfriend, only to reject him once he is snared. The irony is that by doing so she cleanses her bespattered public image.

The next story, "A Nice Quiet Place" (31 May 1930), also has Josephine vamping a desirable young man, this time while banished by

67

her parents to a dull country resort, but she has to return home before her conquest is complete. After staging a scene at a wedding, she catches a train back to the resort, under the innocent guise of pursuing the simple life. In "A Woman With a Past" (6 September 1930) the motif of irony turns against her; she loses a supremely desirable man to a more stable, wholesome woman and loses her reputation as well, on this occasion unjustly, when a man who revolts her holds her against her will in a locked room. The story also foreshadows her ultimate accounting; in her failure to win the man she wants, she realizes she is investing more than she is reaping, while growing increasingly blasé about life and love. The story ends, however, with yet another casual contact, demonstrating that she has not fully learned her lesson.

The fourth installment in the series, "A Snobbish Story" (29 November 1930), interrupts the pattern of Josephine's growth by turning to the theme of class differences. The aristocratic heroine finds herself pursued by a fresh, distinctly un-aristocratic journalist-playwright, flirts with him and the stage, then, after a sequence of complications, rejects both to ally herself "with the rich and powerful of this world forever." Ober noticed the shift in the series and told Fitzgerald, "I didn't like the last Josephine story as well as some of the others but the *Post* seemed to like it very much" (*As Ever*, p. 173).

Fitzgerald was apparently running out of ideas for Josephine, since the next and last story in the series did not appear until 15 August 1931, only after its theme had been worked out in a number of other stories he contributed in the intervening months. Entitled "Emotional Bankruptcy," it traces Josephine's final anguished discovery that she has spent all her emotional resources, epitomized as she kisses her ideal man and feels nothing. Despite the poignance of the moment and the heroine's desperate cries for help, the *Post* reader must have thought her fate morally justified, as no doubt did Fitzgerald. She was not the first wild woman—or man—in the *Post*'s pages to pay for excesses in physical and emotional exhaustion; examples go back at least as far as Nalbro Bartley's "The Gorgeous Girl," a serial of early 1920. Furthermore, as noted above, the first years of the Depression lent themselves particularly well to fiction on the theme of retribution for one's sins of excess.

Most of the stories that Fitzgerald alternated with Josephine treat this theme in some way, though not all. In fact, Fitzgerald's first non-Josephine publication to appear during the series was not even written by him but by his wife Zelda. "A Millionaire's Girl" (17 May

The Price of Paradise

1930) is a smartly cynical look at a rocky marriage, but while the matter is Fitzgerald's the manner is not; in the place of the usual dramatic scenes and dialogue punctuated by authorial commentary that characterized his *Post* fiction, this story is virtually all narrative. That the editors accepted it without flinching gives some evidence of their almost unquestioning loyalty to the author at this time.

"The Bridal Party," published 9 August 1930, goes back to motifs of the *Gatsby* era, as a young man who loses his lover to the wealthy suddenly inherits a fortune. As in *Gatsby*, money alone does not speak loudly enough; the woman remains with his rival, even though the latter has lost his wealth in the Crash. More in line with the major motifs of this period is the next non-Josephine tale, "One Trip Abroad" (11 October 1930). Depicting a couple much like the Fitzgeralds who debauch themselves in Europe, it has received much attention by critics. Despite a hint of supernaturalism—the Kellys watch their decline take place in a doppelgänger couple—this piece must be regarded as one of Fitzgerald's more serious efforts of 1930, and yet another in the new mode of guilt and remorse. Of "The Hotel Child" (31 January 1931), on the other hand, little can and should be said. It shares with other Fitzgerald stories of this period the European setting and with the Josephine series the misjudged reputation of the young female protagonist. The *Post* accepted it without hesitation despite some reservations about its plotlessness and shady characters (*As Ever*, p. 175).

Amazingly and unpredictably, Fitzgerald's next was the best he ever published in *The Saturday Evening Post*, and one of the best short stories—some say *the* best—of his career. "Babylon Revisited," the opening feature of the 21 February 1931 number, brings together again the European setting and the guilt and retribution theme of the early thirties, but without the overt moral device of "One Trip Abroad." The story succeeds in large part through technique. The writing is focused and restrained, and instead of charting the entire course of his hero's dissolution and gradual recovery, the sort of thing Fitzgerald too often did, he concentrates on a few dramatic scenes within a restricted time frame, filling in the background as the plot unfolds. We watch the protagonist Charlie Wales drift among his old, and now nearly abandoned, Paris haunts; we see him engaged in tender moments with his daughter Honoria and in tense confrontations with the hostile sister-in-law that has custody of the young girl. We learn from Charlie's memories of his having locked his wife out in a snowstorm during a drunken quarrel and of her later death from apparently unrelated circumstances.

In an artistically understated climax, Charlie's past overtakes him once more when two former fellow wastrels turn up during a particularly crucial encounter with his sister-in-law; in the following scene he discovers that she is going to deny him custody of his child for at least another six months. The story ends with Wales promising to himself to try again, to continue to fight to overcome the past, since "he wanted his child, and nothing was much good now, beside that fact." One striking aspect of this story new to Fitzgerald is the protagonist's desire to bury the past rather than exhume and relive it like so many characters in the *Gatsby* phase. In addition, Wales accepts responsibility instead of running away from it, and he faces adversity with strength and determination more than self-pity.

As superior as this story clearly is in comparison to the others Fitzgerald was publishing around this time, one should not, as some critics do, assume it a misfit within the *Post* format. It shares a surprising number of motifs with the work of other *Post* writers, even beyond the above-noted association of the Boom with wild spending, alcoholism, and the break-up of the family, and the Crash with penance and punishment. For instance, the Hergesheimer story "Fine Apparel," which appeared one week before "Babylon Revisited" in the 14 February 1931 number, opens with its protagonist George Tait sitting alone in a room of his massive house reflecting upon the recent past: the years of success, wild parties, drinking, and throwing money away on wine, cigars, "fine apparel," and other material vices, and then the subsequent devastation and destitution, with nothing put away for the future. He too lost his wife to the elements as a result of Boom thoughtlessness; she contracted pneumonia when her flimsy dress was soaked in a rainstorm following a typical twenties party. He too is estranged from his offspring, in this case two teenaged daughters—part of the price paid for the sins of the previous decade. Hergesheimer's story also ends on a note of resolve; Tait decides to sell off his frippery, move to smaller quarters, and try to put together his family and his future. As he tells himself, "He would never again make the mistake of complacency."

Though the parallels between Fitzgerald's own circumstances and "Babylon Revisited" are clear to students of his life and work, these are irrelevant within the context of *The Saturday Evening Post*, which was providing in 1931 a forum for the national second thoughts sparked by the economic crisis. Stories like Fitzgerald's and Hergesheimer's implied that the lesson had been learned, that Americans were willing, indeed anxious, to inter the mistakes of the past, get on their feet, and proceed with the business of living. Yet, beyond the thematic suitability of "Babylon" to the *Post*, the fact that such a well-controlled, well-written, un-melodramatic story could appear in the honored position of the first feature in the magazine's pages should be proof that the editors bore no hostility to literary value *per se*. Reflecting the stand of many critics, Henry Dan Piper insists that the *Post* accepted the story with the complaint "that Fitzgerald was writing too much about Europe and that [the magazine] wanted more good one-hundred percent American backgrounds in his stories!" (p. 171).

In fact, this complaint actually came to Ober in response to the three stories Fitzgerald sent to the *Post* after "Babylon," to wit, "Flight and Pursuit," "A New Leaf," and "Indecision." None of these are remarkably good, and as in several other stories he had written since the Basil series the author leaves himself open to the charge that he was using European atmosphere to fill in for plot and characterization. "Indecision," for instance, his next piece to appear (16 May 1931), places a man in Europe between the two women he loves. After one farcical scene at a costume ball where he strives to avoid both, he pursues one in vain, only to encounter her fortuitously the next day and propose. If "New Leaf" (4 July 1931) seems any better, it is because of the pathos of Dick Ragland's inability to overcome his alcoholism coupled with the modern reader's knowledge of the author's parallel situation. Ragland's apparent suicide at the end of the story may seem to "evade *Post* restrictions," as Matthew Bruccoli believes (*Bits of Paradise*, New York: Scribner's, 1973, p. 10), but as we have seen it was not an unprecedented fictional motif in the months following the Crash. Fitzgerald uses it again in "Between Three and Four" (5 September 1931), a story that substitutes melodrama for pathos. Set in New York in the early Depression, it details the effect of guilt on a man who fires a woman in revenge for her having rejected his attentions years before. Burdened with the increasing delusion that she has killed herself and that her ghost is haunting him, he jumps out of a window. In a twist ending, it is revealed that she was merely waiting outside his office on other business.

Fitzgerald made use of the Depression formulas again in "A Change of Class," published shortly thereafter on 26 September 1931, in which a barber wins wealth on the bull market, only to lose his wife, his virtue, and his fortune in by now predictable fashion; in the end, he returns contentedly to barbering. The subject of class also forms the core of "A Freeze-Out" (9 December 1931). Here Fitzgerald returns to the world of the upper-class—this year still the frequent territory of writers Marquand and Hergesheimer, among others—with a story of snobbishness overcome by romantic love. "Diagnosis" (20 February 1932) returns to the guilt and retribution theme, though in this case the protagonist does actually free himself from the past by attempting to confess his wrongdoing to the injured party, his half brother, only to discover that he was never really at fault at all.

Next appeared "Flight and Pursuit" (14 May 1932), which Fitzgerald had sold to the *Post* the year before. It belongs to the earlier European sequence and traces a woman's rejection in love, subsequent marriage to the wrong man, and divorce, followed by her dissipation in Europe. When she lands in a sanatorium with tuberculosis, the man who originally rejected her takes on her care. Only when he is reported missing at sea does she realize she still loves him. In a last-minute twist of good fortune, he returns safely to her arms. This story demonstrates what was wrong with much of Fitzgerald's work at the time. The plot, for one thing, is spread so thin over time and place—he had not continued to employ the tight structure of "Babylon Revisited," though nothing prevented him from doing so—that it tends to evaporate, deserving in this case the editors' charge of plotlessness. And if authorial comment seems less in evidence here than it was in his stories of the twenties, so does the concern for the characters it often encouraged. Furthermore, the sudden happy ending proved to be an ill omen; while not particularly common in the stories of this chapter of his career, this unfortunate practice would plague the stories of his later period.

Fitzgerald's next story, "Family in the Wind" (4 June 1932), is an unusual one for this author, though perfect for the *Post*; Lorimer placed it first in the issue, accompanied by an almost full-page illustration of a tornado with inset portraits of the four main characters. Set in a small southern town peopled with appropriate types, it focuses on one Dr. Forrest Janney, another in Fitzgerald's line of professionals who have thrown their lives and careers away on drink. When tragedy in the form of two tornadoes assaults the town where he has taken refuge, the doctor, however, finds he still has sufficient resources to heal, save lives, and win back some self-respect. He appears well on the way to full recovery when, at the story's conclusion, he takes on the care of a little girl orphaned by the storm.

"Family in the Wind" deserves the accusations of melodrama and sentimentality that some critics have leveled at it. Nevertheless, most commentators acknowledge that the story succeeds on its own terms; it is *Post* fiction, but it is *good Post* fiction. Fitzgerald evinces considerable descriptive skill in conveying the spirit of the early Depression, and the characterizations and dialogue are convincing. The plot moves swiftly, making use of the technique of focusing on a narrow time frame that informs most of his best work. It is also true, unfortunately, that this was "the last noteworthy story he would write for *The Saturday Evening Post*" (Piper, p. 168).

The story that followed, "The Rubber Check" (6 August 1932), uses Fitzgerald's old motif, best handled in *Gatsby*, of a middle-class man intruding on upper-class society. In this instance he is "frozen out" after being forced to write a bad check. He loses his girl, gains a fortune in business, then loses that in the Crash. He ends up, ironically, at the bottom of the social ladder, kneeling in dirt tending cabbage, though the aristocratic daughter of the landholder seems, in the story's final passage, to offer the young man hopes of something better. Nothing better turns up in Fitzgerald's last two stories of 1932, however. "What a Handsome Pair!" (27 August 1932) traces the history of a marriage between two beautiful, talented people who end up destroying one another, contrasted with an unlikely but happy match between a pianist and a working-class Irishwoman. "One Interne" (5 November 1932) looks ahead to later work in its painfully light romance formula and the use of medical personnel as main characters. In this, the intern of the title falls in love with a nurse engaged to a surgeon, but wins her somehow after behaving childishly during an intestinal attack. Despite its overall weakness and silliness, Lorimer placed it not too far from the front of the issue.

Fitzgerald also published two pieces of fiction in 1932 outside the *Post*. The first was the extremely poor "Six of One—," in the February issue of *Red Book*. It simply pits six privileged and wealthy young men against six from the middle and working classes; the latter succeed in life through hard work while the former dissipate themselves. Though the theme was familiar enough to the *Post*, the story was either too wooden for the editors' tastes or too bad to allow Fitzgerald to offer it to them. On the other end of the artistic spectrum is "Crazy Sunday," an excellent story of humiliation, redemption, and infidelity set in the fast-living world of Hollywood. Too cynical and realistic for the mass magazines, which feared jeopardizing their relationships with the movie capital, it ended up in the October issue of *The American Mercury*.

One of the magazines that had turned down "Crazy Sunday" was *Cosmopolitan*, which had been begging Ober for Fitzgerald stories since 1931. They went so far as to offer $5,000 per story and fewer restrictions on subject matter than the *Post*. But Fitzgerald feared jeopardizing his secure berth with Lorimer and let the opportunity go. He also passed up similar offers from *Collier's* and *Liberty*. *College Humor* and *Scribner's*, though interested as well in Fitzgerald's work, paid too little to interest him, though Zelda continued to publish under her husband's name in *College Humor* and an essay of Fitzgerald's, "Echoes of the Jazz Age," did appear in the November 1931 *Scribner's*. By and large, however, he remained a loyal *Post* author through 1933, and the magazine's editors returned his loyalty with preferential treatment.

Being a part of the *Post* stable had its advantages in the lean years of the early Depression. Increasingly, Lorimer's regulars dominated the magazine's pages, often with extended serials and character series. The years 1931-1932 saw the initiation of serials or series by Marquand (about a modern family of aristocrats), Hergesheimer (on high society in Palm Beach), Clarence Budington Kelland (about an English lord in America), Guy Gilpatric (with a tough, shrewd Scottish skipper named Glencannon), Montague Glass (with a Jewish shyster), and F. Britten Austin (on famous vamps of history), among others, as well as the continuation from the twenties of such long-running favorites as Arthur Train's clever lawyer Mr. Tutt, William Hazlett Upton's bumbling tractor salesman Alexander Potts, and Hugh Wiley's black crapshooter Wildcat.

The virtual hegemony of regular authors and regular characters probably reflected the financial situation. Predictably, the magazine had lost a good deal of advertising in the first years of the Depression and the nature of what remained had changed. Automobiles and their accessories, throughout the twenties the leading advertisers in the *Post*'s pages, had shrunk to second place, behind the more practical and affordable toiletries and health aids. Lorimer even broke a longstanding policy by introducing cigarette ads. With less revenue going in, the magazine took fewer chances with the material presented to readers, and nothing could be more dependable than repeatedly using characters and authors of proven popularity.

The Price of Paradise

Unfortunately, Fitzgerald's status at the *Post* did not prevent the editors from cutting his price per story first to $3,000 then $2,500, making 1932 the worst financial year of his career so far. Late that year he briefly abandoned *Post* fiction to return to *Tender Is the Night*, the novel that had been in the background for most of a decade. He got well into the final revision before running short of money and resuming his work for the *Post*. He found himself desperate not only for cash but for story ideas as well. As a group his 1933 stories are poorer than most he turned out for the magazine, and they represented the beginning of the end of his *Post* career. Even as he moved toward the 1934 publication of *Tender Is the Night*, his fourth novel, Fitzgerald was approaching the nadir of his professional life.

IV.
FALSE STARTS AND FALSE ENDINGS

Fitzgerald's last year (1933) as a member of the *Post* stable commenced with the 4 March publication of his first non-fiction piece for the magazine since 1924. In "One Hundred False Starts" he describes, with light, desperate humor that has taken on in retrospect a certain poignancy, the problems he was having at this time as a professional writer with digging up and developing ideas. Most of the essay is given over to the rediscovery of snippets of plot, characterization, and dialogue that never grew into stories. He also describes his own bad behavior in a hospital that led to an unnamed story, undoubtedly "One Interne." At the end of the piece, he quotes Joseph Conrad on the task of authorship, while promising to labor on in the hope of occasional success amid the wasted motion and false starts.

This article accurately characterizes this phase of Fitzgerald's career, a period marked by a growing artificiality in Fitzgerald's fiction, matched by an increasing malaise in his personal life, which was then plagued by mounting debts, alcohol, disease, and Zelda's now apparently permanent disorder. If his stories were able to get past the false starts, they were marred with false endings. In 1933 he produced four *Post* stories, his total output for the year except for the essay "Ring" commissioned by Edmund Wilson for *The New Republic* upon Lardner's death. None of the stories add anything interesting to the author's canon. The first, "On Schedule" (18 March), has a few autobiographical touches—the male protagonist raising his daughter single-handedly, for instance—but the focus is on his obsession with running his household on a strict timetable to facilitate his scientific work. The conflict hinges on the loss of some schedules and important notes and the madcap endeavor to put matters right. At the last moment, the papers turn up.

"More Than Just a House" (24 June) explores an aristocratic family haunted by their past, much like Marquand's Dansel family that was then appearing in series form in the magazine. Though Fitzgerald uses his usually successful involved narrator-observer, in this case a young man who falls in love serially with each of the family daughters, he again makes the mistake of extending the story over several years. Finally, after the family members have married, died, or faded away one by one, the narrator finds the last daughter alone in the empty, foreclosed upon mansion and proposes. "I Got Shoes" (23 September) concerns an actress's obsession with saving all of the shoes she has ever owned, the improbable result of an incident in her poorer childhood, when her mother's inability to buy her new shoes caused the girl serious foot injuries. She conquers this obsession only at the story's end upon accepting the proposal of a well-to-do explorer.

"The Family Bus" (4 November) details a family's history with an automobile (Fitzgerald could have titled the story "More Than Just a Car"). In the first two-thirds of the narrative, the "bus" figures in a family death, a family scandal, and the young hero's humiliation at college. Years later, as a successful businessman in the auto industry, he learns of the car's real economic value. What follows is a farcical sequence in which he and an old lover race round trying to track down the auto, succeed, and apparently fall in love again. Also in 1933, Fitzgerald attempted to establish another series, this one based on an intern, possibly the character of "One Interne," with a story entitled "What to Do About It." It was apparently so bad and so carelessly done that not only did the *Post* reject it, but *Red Book* and *Cosmopolitan* as well. Coming so soon after his reduction in pay, this and other rejections prompted Fitzgerald to begin seeking new markets elsewhere.

He was clearly overreaching for ideas, in the process moving too far from the emotions and experiences that produced his best fiction. It was not true that the *Post* was unwilling to accept more along the lines of his older work, despite the belief of some critics that "for most of mid-Depression America, Fitzgerald's 1920 formula love stories were as old-fashioned as Lorimer's political opinions" (Piper, p. 169). Other writers continued to work quite successfully in modes Fitzgerald had all but abandoned at the end of the twenties. For instance, the story that appeared immediately after "The Family Bus" in the magazine's pages, "Winter with the Cigales," by Davis Gray, describes a situation much like that of "The Popular Girl" of 1922, except that the unfortunate woman has been made destitute by the Crash and that, instead of an extended ploy, she struggles with the decision to look for a job before being saved at the last minute by an old boyfriend. The same issue also continued a serial by Alice Duer Miller set among the wealthy of New York and a college football story, other former formula settings for Fitzgerald's fiction. Such stories seemed "old-fashioned" only to the highbrow set, who were then more interested in the Depression-era Marxism of John Dos Passos and Michael Gold.

The *Post* was making use of a few new formulas as well. Increasingly popular, reflecting the vogue growing in the country at large, was the murder mystery, which lent itself particularly well to serials and series characters. Agatha Christie's "Murder on a Calais Coach," a serial that later became the novel *Murder on the Orient Express*, appeared alongside Fitzgerald's 1933 stories. In fact, almost every second serial that ran in the *Post* in the mid-thirties was a murder mystery, and such *Post* regulars as Marquand and Mary Roberts Rinehart made the form their own. While Fitzgerald hardly had the temperament for this genre, it is surprising that he did not pursue another for which he was particularly well equipped: the Hollywood story. Hollywood, movies, and movie people had grown in popularity as subjects for fiction and articles since the late twenties, until by 1935 barely an issue of the *Post* emerged without at least one piece concerning the movie capital. The only Hollywood story Fitzgerald had published in the early thirties was "Crazy Sunday." Though it was too "sensational" for the *Post*, Fitzgerald certainly could have produced Hollywood stories as acceptable and at least competent as those appearing in the magazine at that time.

Instead, he pursued another relatively new *Post* theme: the effects of the Depression on American life. "No Flowers" (21 July 1934) compares, through fantasy and flashback, three generations of college proms—the genteel elegance of the turn of the century, the wasteful wildness of the early flapper era, and the austerity of the mid-Depression. Not so pointed is "New Types" (22 September 1934), in which a man returns to the United States, having been overseas for both the Boom and the Crash, and gets involved with a daughter of decayed, poverty-ridden aristocracy who seems to sell soul and all for cash, only to reveal the money was needed for an operation for her paralyzed husband. When the husband dies after surgery, the observer-protagonist steps in with the promise of future romance. In both of these, the Depression-era heroine is far more earnest, pragmatic, and spiritually strong than her foremothers and -sisters. His last story of 1934, "Her

Last Case" (3 November), features a young nurse and an older man haunted by his family's past and tormented by his ex-wife. The nurse helps reunite him with his young daughter and breaks her own engagement to commit herself to him. This story contains several of Fitzgerald's mid-Depression motifs: the hard-working, moral new woman of the thirties, the individual plagued by family history, the changing of romantic partners, the single father of a young daughter, and the use of characters in the medical profession.

Fitzgerald had hoped that the 1934 publication of his long-awaited novel *Tender Is the Night* would liberate him from the necessity of keeping the pot boiling with short stories. But the novel's popular reception was, if anything, more disappointing than *Gatsby*'s nearly a decade before. Weary of trying, with increasingly poorer results, to turn out the same old stuff for the *Post*, Fitzgerald sought new territory. While *Scribner's*, for obvious publicity reasons, serialized *Tender* (though only after coming up to the prices offered by *Cosmopolitan* and *Liberty*), Fitzgerald negotiated through Ober with *The Red Book* to do a series of stories built around a fictional ninth-century French count, Philippe de Villfranche. *The Red Book*'s Edwin Balmer was apparently the only editor Ober approached who was willing to take a chance on this idea, and Ober added in a letter to Fitzgerald that "the owners of his magazine were not yet convinced that he was not partially crazy in buying these stories..." (*As Ever*, p. 206). Though medieval romance was not unpublishable at this time, it was not thought of as one of Fitzgerald's specialties. As Ober explained to him,

> ...you have a reputation for writing a very modern story. If an editor wants an authoratative [sic] story about modern society, you are one of the first authors that would come to his mind. The result is that when a reader picks up a magazine with one of your stories in it and finds a story about the ninth century he is going to be shocked. (*As Ever*, p. 206)

Only three installments of Philippe were published before Balmer's second thoughts caused him to drop the series. A fourth installment which the editor simply held back was not published until the year following Fitzgerald's death. The first story, "In the Darkest Hour" (October 1934) sets the tone for the rest. Philippe returns to the French community of his birth after growing up in Moorish Spain. He finds the people disorganized, disease-ridden, poor, and subject to frequent assaults by Viking invaders. The tough-talking count, modeled on Hemingway, whips the peasants, who all speak the patois of American tenant farmers, into a militia that trounces the invaders and establishes a primitive government with himself as the head.

The subsequent tales—"The Count of Darkness" (June 1935), "The Kingdom in the Dark" (August 1935), and the posthumously printed "The Gods of Darkness" (November 1941)—follow the continuation of Philippe's violent career of expansion and consolidation in a chaotic land, for which he pays the price, ultimately losing his lover to another. Though the stories are perhaps better plotted and on one level more interesting than his contemporaneous *Post* fiction, Fitzgerald was completely out of his element in ninth-century France. Philippe seems out of place as well amid *Red Book*'s usual fare: mysteries by Ellery Queen, Agatha Christie, and Arthur Somers Roche, romantic comedies by the like of Octavus Roy Cohen and Thorne Smith (author of *Topper*), adventures set among modern cowboys, explorers, and aviators, and other assorted tales of love, sports, and humor. Fitzgerald's work was exceptional, while not exceptionally good.

The year 1935 also saw Fitzgerald place stories in two other minor markets, though these too were among his worst pieces. The June issue of *McCall's* carried "The Intimate Strangers," in which a young American woman married to an aging French marquis has an affair with a vigorous young American, then marries him years later after her first husband dies. Unfortunately, the young man is now prone to alcoholic binges and long absences from home. At the conclusion the woman discovers that a part of him is still devoted to his late former wife—the first the woman and the reader has heard of her. Through tender understanding the heroine reasserts her love for him. *Liberty*, which in Maxwell Perkins's words had grown "horribly cheap" under the sensationalist Bernarr Macfadden (*Dear Scott*, p. 184), published a horribly cheap story by Fitzgerald in the 8 June issue entitled "The Passionate Eskimo." It begins by describing a group of Eskimos on exhibit at the Chicago World's Fair, then dissipates in plotlessness. Fitzgerald also managed to place one story in the *Post* in 1935. "Zone of Accident," published 13 July, concerns a Hollywood actress who falls in love with a doctor while being treated in a hospital. The doctor permits the actress to have his girlfriend sent to Hollywood so that he will be free to remain with the actress. It is not the worst of his stories of this time, but it comes nowhere near his best work.

One other market of 1935 began as a minor one, though it would come to dominate Fitzgerald's magazine career in the closing years of his life. The periodical in question, *Esquire*, came into existence in October 1933, born of the collaboration of three men—David Smart, William Weintraub, and Arnold Gingrich—who had already worked together for some years putting out a men's clothing trade paper called *Apparel Arts*. In response to a request from a major men's store for some sort of advertising booklet that could be given away or sold to customers, these entrepreneurs began experimenting with the idea of interspersing men's fashions with articles on sports and other features that would give the total layout a "hair-chested" image (Arnold Gingrich, *Nothing But People*, New York: Crown, 1971, p. 81). By the time they had assembled a format "substantial enough to deodorize the lavender whiff coming from the mere presence of fashion pages" (Gingrich, p. 81), they found they had a full-sized magazine that could sell for no less than fifty cents, a steep price in the middle of the Depression when *The Saturday Evening Post* and its competitors were selling for a nickel a copy.

By this time the new periodical was envisioned as a quarterly combining the sophistication of *Town and Country*, the intellectual and literary progressivism of *The American Mercury*, and the light, satirical wit of *Vanity Fair*. Gingrich, who would be the magazine's editor, began scouring the country's artistic and literary centers for talent. The first major author he contacted was one he had long admired—Ernest Hemingway. Hemingway proved wholly enthusiastic about the new venture and agreed to submit something for each issue, usually a journalistic "letter" on his hunting and fishing activities, for twice the top price paid to anyone else, which meant for Hemingway an initial $200 per piece. A number of other authors, such as Ezra Pound, John Dos Passos, and Morley Callaghan, fell in behind Hemingway. Gingrich remembers the latter as "the greatest single friend the magazine had in its beginning days" (p. 274).

Immediately following Hemingway in their enthusiasm for the new magazine and their ability to corral authors for it were Gingrich's friend George Jean Nathan and his colleague Mencken. Nathan not only contributed to the first issues himself, but brought in Sinclair Lewis and Edgar Lee Masters. Mencken encouraged Theodore Dreiser to become an early and regular contributor, and he was responsible, according to Gingrich, for bringing Fitzgerald into the magazine as well. In many ways, considering the high tone of *Esquire*, it is fitting that Fitzgerald should have been brought full circle at this point in his career by the man who was the earliest mentor of his professional life.

With its debut, *Esquire* proved an immediate success. The original plan to distribute it in men's stores had to be abandoned in favor of general newsstand and subscription sales, and the quarterly became a monthly with the January 1934 number. The cover of this issue introduced "Esky," the mustached little man that became the magazine's symbol, as a colorful clay figure climbing into a champagne glass to celebrate the December repeal of Prohibition. The periodical was large-sized, nearly the dimensions of the *Post*—more than 125 pages thick, slick and bright with colored artwork, full-page cartoons, and advertising photos. Each issue of the first months of 1934 opened with a brief article by Hemingway from places like Africa or Cuba, heavy with manly humor and the odor of the kill, followed by a great mélange of fiction, non-fiction, and humor, penned by contemporary literati and lesser lights.

The issue that first carried Fitzgerald's name, May 1934, is exemplary of the early *Esquire*. Appearing in Hemingway's usual spot as first feature is the article "'Show Mr. and Mrs. F. to Number—,'" bylined "F. Scott and Zelda Fitzgerald" though credited to Zelda alone in Fitzgerald's Ledger. Subtitled "Journal of a thousand and one nights in hotel rooms, in the gilded dawn of the Jazz Age," it consists wholly of year by year descriptive reminiscences of places—hotels, villas, and the like—in which the Fitzgeralds had stayed throughout the twenties. In the fashion of other commercial magazines, the article is strung out through the advertising section in the hinter reaches of the magazine.

Immediately following this is Theodore Dreiser's "Mathewson," the first of a two-part reminiscence about a St. Louis journalist under whom Dreiser had worked at the turn of the century. Next comes a full-page color display of various trout flies leading off an article on trout fishing, then a "satire" by Jim Tully, a regular, about a barnyard revolt, an article about the inability of France or Germany to fight another war, a story by Ivan Bunin about "that time of my life when the passions of youth survive only in the memory," an article called "The Art of Bartending" about the colorful Paris of the exiles, a story by regular Manuel Komroff featuring a subconscious dialogue between two criminals dying of gunshot wounds, and a humorous article on bridge.

Highly typical of the early *Esquire* short story is the one that follows, Morley Callaghan's "The Girl Who Was Easy." It opens at the counter of a cheap restaurant, with two men, Bernie and Olsen, eyeing a waitress. The earthy, cynical Olsen urges Bernie to make a play for her, positive that she is "easy." Bernie refuses to believe him but shyly begins to court her on subsequent visits. Eventually, with his friend's somewhat coarse urging, he takes her home. She lets him into her apartment, where she reveals she is engaged but kisses him anyway before sending him away. Bernie, now certain he was right about her virtue, tells Olsen all, but Olsen convinces him her willingness to kiss him indicates her willingness to go further. Bernie feels furious at this destruction of his romantic vision, but suppresses his desire to lash back.

This piece certainly cannot be confused with the school of fiction prominent in the *Post* and most other general audience magazines of the time. For one thing, it is much shorter—about 2500 words, or about one-fourth the length of the average *Post*-style story. Related to the brevity is the de-emphasis of plot; Callaghan's story possesses very few scenes, which take place within sharply limited parameters of time and place. Nothing particularly dramatic happens, although the story is dramatic in another sense, that is, its action is depicted by way of the words and deeds of the characters instead of through dense narrative and authorial intervention. The story does not describe significant changes in any of the characters but works instead toward a specific and quite subtle emotional effect. Furthermore, although Bernie is the main character and by and large sympathetic, the reader is not induced to identify with him. All of these features—the "dramatic" style, the de-emphasis of plot, the restricted but distanced point of view, the subtlety and irony—are characteristic of the "modern" short story.

Virtually all of the stories in the May 1934 *Esquire* share these qualities, though some tend to the melodramatic and sensational. Among the latter is William McFee's "Little Angevine," featuring an opium-addicted sailor, a French prostitute, blackmail, gang violence, and murder. A more painfully effective tale is "The Folks at Home" by Langston Hughes, in which a black violinist with a European reputation returns to his Missouri home with consumption. He tends to his mother, befriends the cultured few in his small town, but is branded an "uppty [sic] nigger" by the rabble and ends up swinging, naked and mutilated, from a tree.

Such fiction, with its brutal naturalism and its cold cynicism, most resembles that pioneered by Mencken in the later *Smart Set* and *American Mercury*. But even while borrowing from the avant-garde of an earlier decade, *Esquire*'s writers proved themselves to be on top of

The Price of Paradise

more recent trends. For example, J. L. Campbell's "Shooting at the Moon," also in the May 1934 issue, is a straight-faced comedy in which a destitute French streetwalker fools a wealthy man into making her his mistress. Though thematically this story also harks back to *The Smart Set*, stylistically it shows the influence of Hemingway, as in this passage:

> The man turned and passed the bench again. He looked at her. He had a full black beard. Louise hummed to herself. She was glad she had remained seated. It is always better to be pursued than to pursue. She wondered where he came from. He did not look Parisian.

And so on.

The other stories in this issue of *Esquire* include an episode in which a pair of dope-peddlers save a girl from white slavers, a suspense story about a man trapped in a cave, a story set among boxers in Victorian England and another among Americans in Holland, and two humorous pieces, one about the struggle of an American in Paris with French bureaucracy, and the other about a burlesque entertainer getting the better of her entrepreneurs. Amid the fiction are articles on new stock regulations, new rules of etiquette, the marketing of motion pictures, the legal career of then Attorney General Homer Cummings, baseball, tennis, horse-racing, and pre-Columbian art, as well as regular features such as Gilbert Seldes on "The Lively Arts" (i.e., mass entertainment), Burton Roscoe on books, and John V. A. Weaver on the theatre. Sprinkled through the latter half of the magazine are displays of men's fashions, full-page cartoons, and ads for clothing, liquor, toiletries, a few resort and sporting areas, and *The American Mercury*, all oriented toward the well-rounded, well-funded gentleman in the prime of life.

The Fitzgeralds appeared in the subsequent two issues of the magazine, in June with the second half of "'Show Mr. and Mrs. F. to Number—'" and in July with "Auction—Model 1934," like the first article a retrospective glance at the previous decade. Also like the first, it was the work of Zelda Fitzgerald. These pieces were printed in the company of articles by Hemingway on hunting, Dreiser on journalism, Bertrand Russell on free thought, and Gilbert Seldes on Ring Lardner, and ahead of stories by D. H. Lawrence, H. E. Bates, Lord Dunsany,

Guido D'Agostino, and Luigi Pirandello, poetry by Edgar Lee Masters, and other pieces by Ezra Pound, André Maurois, and George Jean Nathan, though the majority of contributors were not so distinguished. In the remaining months of its first year, *Esquire* would publish more from the above-mentioned authors, as well as material from Ben Hecht, Conrad Aiken, Leon Trotsky, Harpo Marx, Edwin Balmer, Havelock Ellis, and newcomer William Saroyan—some of whom, like Hecht, Ellis, and Saroyan, would join the ranks of early regulars.

The literati, old and new, were certainly not flocking to *Esquire* for the money; by the end of 1934, the magazine remained unable to pay anyone more than $150, with the important exception of Hemingway. *Esquire* did provide these authors something that other periodicals could not, however: a relatively free hand regarding subject matter and its means of presentation. While this practice meant that a great deal crept into the magazine reminiscent of the "sensational" mode of *Liberty* and *Collier's*—stories of streetwalkers, sinister murders, and life in the demimonde—it also permitted the publication of much fine work that was too earthy, too graphic, too profound or subtle, or simply too unusual for the general run of slick magazines.

To the select group of regulars who were already well-established writers, the group including Hemingway, Dreiser, Nathan, Dos Passos, and Fitzgerald, Gingrich gave carte blanche; he welcomed anything that came under their bylines, be it fiction or non-fiction, aesthetic, personal, or political. Most of these writers generally opted for the essay over the story, undoubtedly finding the opportunity to express themselves openly without the mask of fiction too good to forego. Gingrich and his magazine had also become famous for the "straight-talk," "man-to-man" approach, evident in the personal voices taken by the above-named authors in such typical items as Dreiser's "You, the Phantom," a philosophical discussion concerning man as a product of a naturalistic universe, Nathan's "Sweet Faces and Foul Minds," a disquisition on the greater propensity of women for reading sexual connotations into things, and Hemingway's "Defense of Dirty Words." Such expository pieces, particularly from these three authors, could be found frequently near the front cover of the magazine.

Fitzgerald's first solo appearance in *Esquire* was also an essay; entitled "Sleeping and Walking" and published in December 1934, it concerns the author's increasing struggles with insomnia, and though half-humorous in tone it looks ahead to the deeply personal pieces Fitzgerald would write for the periodical a year later. The January and

February number of 1935 carried Fitzgerald's first fiction for the magazine, respectively, "The Fiend" and "The Night before Chancellorsville." The former is a tale of diabolical revenge somewhat in the vein of Nathaniel Hawthorne. Its protagonist, Crenshaw, haunts the jail cell of the man who has murdered his wife, tormenting him. When the criminal dies, however, Crenshaw discovers that he has lost the only meaningful human contact he had. The story shares with other *Esquire* fiction its diminutive length and a relatively stripped style, though it features the sinister melodrama and the heavy naturalistic irony of the magazine's more second-rate work. It shares with "The Night Before Chancellorsville" a ninteenth-century setting and a departure from the themes and style of the material Fitzgerald was, and is, associated with. Indeed, both stories most resemble the work of nineteenth-century writer Ambrose Bierce.

"Chancellorsville" is narrated in vernacular by a young Northern woman enlisted in General Hooker's battalion of Civil War camp followers. The train on which she is being transported south is commandeered for the movement of wounded soldiers to Washington, and her remarks bespeak her complete insensitivity to the sufferings incurred through battle. Her final comment sums up her attitude, not to mention the story's style: "And in the papers next day they never said anything about how our train got attacked or about us girls at all! Can you beat it?" Though like "The Fiend," this story is generally regarded as mediocre at best (see, for instance, Sklar, p. 301), it at least lacks the former's melodramatic touches. In fact, in its dwelling on a single episode, its restricted point of view, its rendering of dialect, and the ironic distance between the character and the events around her, as well as between the character and the reader, the story is reasonably good *Esquire* fiction.

Indeed, Gingrich included it as a representative piece from the magazine in his 1941 collection *The Bedside Esquire* (New York: Robert M. McBride). Fitzgerald placed both "Chancellorsville" and "The Fiend" in his 1935 collection *Taps at Reveille* as a hedge against the charge that the volume contained "all standardized *Saturday Evening Post* stories, because, whatever can be said about them, they are not that..." (*Dear Scott*, p. 215). Instead, maintains Higgins, they were standardized *Esquire* stories, dispelling any "doubt that he fashioned his stories to fit the magazine for which they were intended" (p. 159). If he did so, however, it was not at the editor's insistence; according to Gingrich, "no ground rules were ever spelled out for Scott Fitzgerald....After [his wife's essays], his contributions were mainly stories, about which there was no prior discussion" (quoted by Higgins, p. 160). Bearing in mind that at this time Fitzgerald was also working on the Philippe series and on the Civil War story that would eventually be published as "The End of Hate," it could be argued that he was merely taking advantage of Gingrich's open-mindedness to experiment with subject matters and techniques that his traditional markets found less than acceptable.

Fitzgerald's only other *Esquire* story for 1935, "Shaggy's Morning," must be regarded as a further experiment with point of view; it is virtually *sui generis* both in the author's *oeuvre* and in *Esquire*. Moving from the cathouse to the doghouse, Fitzgerald creates here a canine narrator who provides a monologue on his matutinal meanderings. The piece is so far outside Fitzgerald's usual parameters, not to mention those of the modern fiction represented in *Esquire*, that it is justifiably overlooked (it is one of the very few stories Fitzgerald's daughter Scottie refuses to reprint). Thus, no one has so far noted its low-level similarities to "The Night Before Chancellorville." The narrator, for one, is insensitive and uncomprehending, in this case toward the accidental death of a fellow hound. Again, the distance between the narrator and reader (here a distance too large to permit any sort of identification) and the irony of the ending (the dog returns to the home of his wounded companion, sees nothing but a crying child, and is unable to grasp that his friend has died) are reminiscent of techniques employed not only in his previous story but in other *Esquire* fiction. In other aspects, however, the piece is well below the standards of both the author and the magazine, and Fitzgerald himself readily admitted to Gingrich upon its appearance in the May issue that it was "rotten" (*Letters*, p. 524).

The year 1935 is often regarded as Fitzgerald's personal and professional nadir. Alongside the generally unfavorable reception of *Tender Is the Night* and *Taps at Reveille*, Piper places his bouts with alcoholism and Zelda's lengthening confinement to institutions (p. 233), to which Eble adds "[d]ebt, cirrhosis of the liver,...and an attack of tuberculosis" (p. 140). His output for the year had been dominated by some of the worst stories, "The Passionate Eskimo," "The Count of Darkness," and "Shaggy's Morning," among others. His agent Harold Ober was growing increasingly reluctant to advance money on unsold or unwritten stories, a practice that had kept Fitzgerald alive for most of his career, and all year long Fitzgerald had been borrowing "dribs and drabs" from Arnold Gingrich "without a single manuscript in the files to show for them" (Gingrich, p. 242). Finally, Gingrich—who had from the first, incidently, dealt directly with Fitzgerald without Ober's professional mediation—suggested that Fitzgerald break his writer's block by writing over and over "I can't write stories of young love for *The Saturday Evening Post* because I can't write stories of young love for *The Saturday Evening Post* because..." etc. (Gingrich, p. 241-42). What Fitzgerald wrote instead was "The Crack-Up," which explained, as Gingrich put it, "as nothing and nobody else ever could, why he couldn't go on writing stories of young love for *The Saturday Evening Post*" (p. 242-43).

"The Crack-Up" and two sequential essays, "Pasting it Together" and "Handle with Care," were published respectively in the February, March, and April issues of 1936. While sharing some imagery with the earlier "Sleeping and Walking"—the "walking dreams of imaginary heroism that were good enough to go to sleep on in restless nights," and that "darkest hour" in early morning which is compared to the "dark night of the soul"—the "Crack-Up" series abandons the pretense of lightness and purports to describe the author's nervous collapse and the slow process of pulling himself back together. The first essay opens with the "general observation" that "the test of a first-rate intelligence is the ability to hold two opposed ideas in the mind at the same time, and still retain the ability to function." Then it discusses in broad, mostly abstract terms his failures, disappointments, and disillusionment, his growing distaste for people and his loss of vitality, all of which he ascribes to have "prematurely cracked."

In "Pasting it Together" he carries on the metaphor of himself as "cracked plate," and in similarly oft-quoted passages talks about his failures in college, his distrust of the rich, and his emotional bankruptcy, complains of the death of the novel, and lists the individuals who had served as his conscience in various fields of concern. "Handle with Care" traces the author's descent into a newly found cynicism; at the end he cuts loose every part of himself but the writer ("I have now at last become a writer only") and draws the parallel between the course of his own career and the national Boom and Bust. He sets himself sullenly against the world, adding however in conclusion: "I will try to be a correct animal though, and if you throw me a bone with enough meat on it I may even lick your hand."

This essay series has probably received more critical attention than anything else Fitzgerald wrote for *Esquire*. Sergio Perosa sums up the consensus that these essays constitute superior work, demonstrating a Fitzgerald who was capable of ruthless self-evaluation without pity or sentimentality, in that he "detached himself, as it were, from his person, and he stood by to contemplate and record" (*The Art of F. Scott Fitzgerald*, Ann Arbor, MI: University of Michigan Press, 1965, p. 141). Much is made of "the particular quality of his writing, here simple and flowing, discursive and easy...reducing the expressive means to the level of conversation" (Perosa, p. 140). The main demurrer comes from Milton Hindus in *F. Scott Fitzgerald: An Introduction and Interpretation* (New York: Holt, 1968). He finds the essay series deficient as personal revelation ("It does not contain enough close-ups of actual experience," p. 90) and too dependent on rhetoric ("...the real emotions and ideas of his confession have to be read through an obscuring mist of verbal artifice," p. 91), though even he calls the series "very superior indeed by more modest standards" (p. 90) and "an important addition not only to Fitzgerald's work but to the best American literature produced at this time" (p. 93).

All this and much more has been attributed to what began as a piece tossed off for $200 in "emergency money." Contemporary response was not so positive. Fitzgerald's colleagues in *Esquire*, particularly Hemingway and Dos Passos, found "The Crack-Up" too maudlin and self-indulgent, while Perkins and Ober both believed that the series had hurt Fitzgerald's reputation and possibly his career. Gingrich, on the other hand, considered the first essay "one of the most memorable the magazine ever received" (p. 242). As a whole, the essays fit perfectly into the "straight-talk" format that characterized all the non-fiction in the magazine, and Gingrich particularly relished honesty of that sort from his name authors. Such openness placed the writers and readers on an equal, more or less "first-name" basis, though it also allowed the latter a rare glimpse of the foibles of the former: Hemingway's snide meanness, Nathan's narrow haughtiness, Dreiser's philosophical pretentiousness, and Ezra Pound's thinly disguised fascism. If Fitzgerald's soul-baring seemed a more overt expression of weakness at the time, it is largely because of his greater self-consciousness.

Ironically, Fitzgerald probably had not expected the exposure he got in *Esquire*; it was difficult for him to take seriously a periodical that paid so little, and he no doubt assumed others felt the same. During this period he was still trying to reassert himself in the better-paying traditional markets. In April 1936, the month that saw the last installation of "The Crack-Up" essays, Fitzgerald published no less than three stories elsewhere, none of them good. *The American Magazine* printed "Fate in Her Hands," about a young woman who barely avoids the doom foretold by a palmreader. *McCall's* carried "Image on the Heart," a story based on an affair Zelda had had some years earlier with a French aviator; here an American man competes with a French aviator for the hand of a young woman the American has supported through college. Finally, after his marriage to the woman, he overcomes his jealousy, despite evidence that she had had a liaison, albeit a chaste one, just before the wedding.

Fitzgerald even placed a story in the 18 April number of the *Post*. Entitled "Too Cute for Words," it represented an attempt on the author's part to initiate a new series, this one about a middle-aged widower and his teenaged daughter Gwen, a relationship modeled on Fitzgerald's own with his daughter Scottie. This story merely describes how the thirteen-year-old girl crashes the Princeton prom, an event her apparently long-suffering father greets with bemused resignation. A second installation, "Inside the House," was published 13 June 1936; it details Gwen's comic comeuppance when she sneaks out to the theatre and has a dreadful time, only to discover when she arrives home that she has missed the opportunity to meet her favorite actress. Happily, her father has arranged in secret for the star to come to dinner the following evening.

Fitzgerald wrote two more Gwen stories, but the *Post* refused them and the series died; they were, according to Lorimer and Ober, too full of inconsistencies and improbabilities. And Ober gave Fitzgerald this warning:

> Mr. Lorimer made it very clear to me that he would not buy another Gwen story unless it were very much better than the last one he bought. In my opinion this story is far below the first two. The story starts very well indeed but it is terribly full of holes and when you try to patch up one hole, another appears somewhere else. I feel it is very important for your future relations with the Post that the next story they see of yours shall be an extremely good one. (*As Ever*, p. 264)

The Gwen story in question here was rewritten and published as "Strange Sanctuary" in *Liberty*, though not until 9 December 1939.

As early as 1933, upon the rejection of Fitzgerald's second interne story, Ober had pointed out to the author that due to the economic situation, "all the magazines have been harder to please...than ever before." He added that of course " a great deal is expected of an author who has written as many fine stories as you have written" (*As Ever*, p. 199). By the end of 1934, Fitzgerald had lost his most loyal supporters at the *Post*; Thomas B. Costain had left the magazine, while George Horace Lorimer was becoming more and more concerned with his administrative position in Curtis, the mother company, and with the purely political features of the periodical. Ober ended up dealing with Lorimer's son Graeme, who did not share with the older editors the long-running admiration of Fitzgerald's fiction. With good reason, Fitzgerald grew increasingly uncertain through the mid-thirties of his ability to write commercial fiction, and he grew more desperate as his work grew worse.

With series characters more prominent than ever in the *Post* (William Faulkner's Sartoris, Tarkington's Little Orvie, Rex Stout's Nero Wolfe, Nelson Reilly Raine's Tugboat Annie, and Marquand's sea-going March family were among the more memorable of the mid-thirties), Fitzgerald attempted to start yet another himself with "'Trouble,'" published 6 March 1937. His last *Post* story, it features a flirtatious young nurse, nicknamed "Trouble," who literally falls for a doctor. When he appears to be involved with another woman, Trouble returns to her wealthy, alcoholic former fiancé, only to throw him over for the doctor when the latter proves to be interested after all. Once more one sees the motifs of Fitzgerald's last *Post* stories: medical personnel, broken engagements, and a hard-working—if overly mischievous—young woman. The *Post* editorial board found the story encouraging because "it shows that Mr. Fitzgerald still can write the simple love story, free of the melodrama that he introduced into his recent manuscripts," *i.e.*, stories which the *Post* had rejected (*As Ever*, p. 275).

It was clear that the magazine still sought the sort of formula love stories that Piper maintains the public had grown tired of by the middle of the Depression. In fact, amid the plethora of mystery, adventure, and action tales that filled its pages, one could still find in the *Post* of the late thirties the type of middle-class and aristocratic romances that had helped make Fitzgerald famous. The week after "'Trouble'" was published, for instance, Joseph Hergesheimer appeared with "Introduction: Waltz: Coda," a story of love set amid the glittering wealth of the cultured ambassadorial set. Fitzgerald's failure to remain acceptable to the editors of the *Post*, therefore, cannot be explained away in terms of a significant swing in taste. The critics who have tried to do so, such as Piper, are confusing the tastes of the middle-brow *Post* readership with those of the intelligentsia, Fitzgerald's other audience, who rejected *Tender Is the Night* because it lacked the kind of class consciousness then in vogue. *Post* readers were more likely among those who made popular such distinctly non-Marxist bestsellers of the Depression as *Anthony Adverse* and *Gone with the Wind*.

Critics sympathetic to Fitzgerald tend too often to take his own observations at face value, and Fitzgerald himself blamed the end of his *Post* career on a change in the preferences of the editors. In a 1940 letter to Zelda, Fitzgerald wrote:

> the man who runs the magazine now [Wesley Winans Stout, who took over as editor upon Lorimer's retirement at the end of 1936] is an up-and-coming young Republican who gives not a damn about literature and who publishes almost nothing except escape stories about the brave frontiersman, etc., or fishing, or football captains. (*Letters*, p. 188)

While there were certainly plenty of such stories in the *Post* of the late thirties, the traditional romance and the Hollywood story persisted in popularity as well. And if these did not satisfy Fitzgerald's definition of literature—or anyone's, for that matter—one must not overlook the fact that William Faulkner continued to publish in the magazine throughout Stout's reign, with stories like "The Bear," published in 1942. By and large, Stout's *Post* was all but identical to Lorimer's, with few changes in editorial personnel or regular contributors. To conclude that Fitzgerald could no longer publish in the periodical because its standards were deteriorating is thus to ignore the facts. If anything, *better* work was expected from the best writers.

Fitzgerald comes closer to the truth in another part of the above-cited letter to Zelda, where he states:

> As soon as I feel I am writing to a cheap specification my pen freezes and my talent vanishes over the hill, and I honestly don't blame them for not taking the

things I've offered to them from time to time in the
past three or four years. (*Letters*, p. 188)

The emphasis should be placed on Fitzgerald's *feeling* that he was writing to cheap specifications. Certainly, a number of his earlier stories that he genuinely liked, such as "Head and Shoulders" and "The Offshore Pirate," are cheap by literary standards, but they possess a seductive vividness lacking in most later stories, particularly those of the mid-thirties. As Fitzgerald told Mencken, "my whole heart was in my first trash"; only later, he maintained, did he start consciously "writing down" (*Letters*, p. 481). The less he respected his *métier* and himself, the more carelessly he wrote. No critic looking at his output from 1933 to 1937, in the *Post* and elsewhere, can deny that the stories in this phase were very bad. Higgins lists their problems:

> ...plots involved, distended and laced with enough implausibility, melodrama and/or sentimentality to vitiate the story; characterization trite and shallow; technique undisciplined and stereotyped. Happy endings are tacked on to stories that by all rules of art and logic should have ended otherwise. (p. 156)

A number of stories from this period did not see print until much later; most of these did not come to light until well after Fitzgerald's death (see Jennifer McCabe Atkinson, "Lost and Unpublished Stories by F. Scott Fitzgerald," *Fitzgerald/Hemingway Annual*, 1971, p. 32-63). A Civil War story written in 1936 and originally titled "Thumbs Up" was declined by thirteen periodicals, including the *Post*, *Woman's Home Companion*, *Redbook*, *McCall's*, *Liberty*, and *American* before appearing as "The End of Hate" in the 22 June 1940 issue of *Collier's*. It was criticized for being too long and disjointed, or too harrowing for sensitive tastes, or "not what the editors expect of you" (*As Ever*, p. 283). A story of torture and redemption through love, it has too many scenes in too little space and lacks emotional depth; the reader does not really feel for or care about the characters. Nevertheless, *Collier's* editor Kenneth Littauer paid him $2,500 for the story and was eager for more. Unfortunately, everything else Fitzgerald sent him was rejected, probably for the same reasons Littauer outlined when he returned the unpublished "Offside Play"—"There is a great deal of good stuff in this story but the action is altogether too

The Price of Paradise

complicated. Unless we are mistaken the whole thing needs to be simplified and very sharply focused" (quoted by Piper, p. 232).

The Saturday Evening Post has often been blamed by critics for the ruination of Fitzgerald's art and his creative exhaustion of the thirties. To a large extent, this attitude perpetuates the stance of his contemporaries. The judgment of the literary set of the thirties toward Fitzgerald is evident in Malcolm Cowley's remark that "Scott Fitzgerald is always described as a representative figure of the 1920s, but the point has to be made that he represented the new generation of ambitious college men rising in the business world much more than he did the writers" (*Exile's Return*, New York: Viking, 1951, p. 292). This assessment is not entirely unfair. It does not take much of a perusal of *The Saturday Evening Post* of the twenties and thirties to see how much Fitzgerald shared thematically and stylistically with many of the regulars of that middle-class organ—writers like Marquand, Hergesheimer, Tarkington, Bernard De Voto, Clarence Budington Kelland, and Mary Roberts Rinehart—much more than he shared with the self-consciously literary authors of the *Dial-New Republic* set. Furthermore, Austin McGiffert Wright, in his detailed study *The American Short Story in the Twenties* (Chicago: University of Chicago Press, 1961), concludes that Fitzgerald was the least experimental, least "modern" writer of any significance in that era in his choice of theme, story form, narrative technique, and style.

What is striking to the modern reader turning to the *Post* of that time, in fact, is how well Fitzgerald fit into the magazine's milieu. And not just the mediocre, obvious hack work, either; some of his best fiction suited the magazine best—the early romances, the Basil stories, "Babylon Revisited." His stories with unhappy endings, like similar stories from other authors, were welcome in the *Post* (though far from frequent), especially when using the accepted motifs: the loss of youth and romance in the late twenties and, in the early thirties, retribution and remorse for past sins of excess. Fitzgerald's period of greatest success with *Post* editors and readers coincided with the years 1927 through 1932, during which he wrote such semi-tragic tales. Since these were the same formulas upon which he based his best novels—*The Great Gatsby* and *Tender Is the Night*—one must conclude it was not the existence of such formulas *per se* that limited Fitzgerald's fiction, but the way he handled them in any particular piece. As *Post* writers went, Fitzgerald had a relatively free hand; he did not accept story ideas from the editors as did other regulars. The factor working most against quality in his *Post* fiction may have been his own oft-expressed embarrassment bred of his desire to be taken seriously by the critics of his own time. To fault the magazine overmuch for Fitzgerald's artistic misjudgments is to do as Mencken warned and blame "the bull for the sins of all the cows."

Although Fitzgerald exercised more thematic flexibility in minor markets such as *Cosmopolitan* and *Redbook*, many of his worst, as well as his best, stories appeared in these. Ironically, his ability to give the magazines what they wanted in the twenties—predominantly, though certainly not limited to, romantic tales of young love—made it that much more difficult for him to cultivate these markets in the late thirties when he was no longer a member of the *Post* stable. Though he still found himself very much in demand, he could not provide the sort of stories the magazines wanted, the sort of stories that made him famous in the twenties. As Fitzgerald complained to Littauer in 1939, "I would be either a miracle man or a hack if I could go on turning out an identical product for three decades" (*Letter*, p. 588). Worse yet, the only short stories he *could* write in the mid-thirties were not only not in the desired categories, they were also not well-crafted even by popular standards. It appeared as if Fitzgerald had lost not only the common touch but his artistic control as well.

The year 1936 was the last in which Fitzgerald made any appreciable money from his fiction. Thereafter he would turn increasingly to Hollywood and the benevolence of editors and friends for his income. As far as periodicals were concerned, from here on he would be an *Esquire* author. Though it offered little in remuneration, the magazine provided Fitzgerald a unique opportunity to experiment with new forms, themes, and techniques, becoming the primary, and virtually the sole, periodical market of his final years.

V.
PASTING IT TOGETHER

In the wake of the qualified success of the "Crack-Up" series, and while he struggled to hang on to his better paying markets, Fitzgerald produced his first significant unbroken run of pieces for *Esquire*. The May 1936 issue contained his "Three Acts of Music," a slight, subtle story which critic James L. W. West III has recently tried to redeem from obscurity ("Fitzgerald and *Esquire*," in *The Short Stories of F. Scott Fitzgerald*, ed. Jackson R. Bryer, Madison, WI: University of Wisconsin Press, 1982, p. 149-166). It consists of three encounters over many years between a doctor and a nurse, unnamed, who pass up a chance at romance in favor of their careers and end up living love vicariously through the music of Youmans, Berlin, and Kern. The sense of loss in this piece is reminiscent of Fitzgerald's fiction of the twenties, though it lacks the vivid characters, plot, and narrative of that fiction. It is thus a much more "modern" story, brief, tight, and understated. It is not, however, the superior effort West maintains it to be.

Far worse is Fitzgerald's contribution to the June 1936 issue, "The Ants of Princeton." A satire in the author's undergraduate vein, it reports on the admission of ants as students to Princeton, and on the ascent of one to football stardom. At best, this piece can be regarded as a further experiment in form and subject matter; at worst as a hasty effort for quick cash. Arnold Gingrich's willingness to accept it was a measure of his faith in Fitzgerald. Pieces almost as bad could be found occasionally under the bylines of other authors, though none of Fitzgerald's stature.

Fitzgerald seemed to be at his best in 1936 when he was working autobiographically. A second trio of very personal pieces followed "The Crack-Up": the "Author" series—"Author's House"

(July), "Afternoon of an Author" (August), and the fictionalized "An Author's Mother" (September). Here, in contrast to the intimate authorial voice of "The Crack-Up," Fitzgerald stands apart from himself and speaks of "the author" in third person. In "Author's House" he opens with the lighter tone of "Sleeping and Walking," then goes on to show a visitor a house that represents metaphorically the author's life and mind. In the middle appears an anecdote that harks back to the misanthropic cynicism of "Handle with Care"—the author cruelly meddles with the hearts of two people who think he is their long-lost brother.

The article is less revealing and more objective than earlier essays, a manner continued in "Afternoon of an Author." The latter is less an experiment in metaphor and more a straight narrative. It details an author's solitary meanderings as he searches for inspiration and also harks back to "Handle with Care," this time to Fitzgerald's oath to strip himself of personal ties, even of personhood, and become "a writer only." The style is likewise stripped, though not wholly without metaphor, as the following passage, in which the author watches a pair of young lovers sitting by themselves, demonstrates:

> Their isolation moved him and he knew he would get something out of it professionally, if only in contrast to the growing seclusion of his life and the increasing necessity of picking over an already well-picked past. He needed reforestation and he was well aware of it, and he hoped the soil would stand one more growth. It had never been the very best soil for he had had an early weakness for showing off instead of listening and observing.

Although the writer is still showing himself off in some sense, the narrator here, unlike that in "Author's House," is completely silent and objective. An even greater aesthetic distance between author-narrator and the reader is apparent in "An Author's Mother," in which "the author," named here Hamilton T. Johnson, remains wholly offstage. During this mere episode, the old lady of the title, modeled on Fitzgerald's mother, seeks a birthday present for her famous son in a book store. She inquires about her favorite genteel romantic poets just before collapsing. She comes to in an ambulance, her mind obviously disordered, then dies in the hospital after confusing her son with the poets. Style, tone, and point of view are tightly controlled, and the character

The Price of Paradise

is drawn pathetically without recourse to sentimentality. Within its limitations, the piece works well and reflects the terse, "masculine" subtleties of *Esquire*'s best fiction.

Two more works of fiction followed quickly upon the "Author" series. The October 1936 *Esquire* carried "'I Didn't Get Over'"; it opens at a college reunion, where the first-person narrator soon introduces one Hibbing, who takes over with a narrative of his own. His is the story of a fellow classmate, Abe, who had come up against a headstrong young captain in training camp, an officer who became responsible for the deaths of several recruits through his stupid acts. The captain, however, managed to blame Abe for everything, and Abe spent the war in federal prison. He was later killed while trying to escape. After this tale is told, all listeners depart but the original narrator, at which time Hibbing reveals that he was the young captain. This story bears most of the best characteristics of typical *Esquire* fiction: the distance between the reader and the characters, the sudden irony and somewhat sinister implications of the conclusion, the relative absence of melodrama or sentimentality, and a conversational, minimal style.

The next piece, published in November and the last of the 1936 sequence, was "'Send Me In, Coach.'" Here Fitzgerald retreats completely from the problem of narrative point of view by casting the story in the form of a playlet; and whereas "'I Didn't Get Over'" contains a narrative within a narrative, "'Send Me In, Coach'" features a play within a play. It focuses on a group of boys at summer camp who are rehearsing a skit with typical genteel romantic motifs about a college football hero who refuses to compromise his honor. Placed in ironic contrast to this ongoing action are two other sub-plots; one concerns a shady deal between the boys' coach and a college athlete, and the other a court case involving the father of one of the boys, eventually leading to the man's suicide. The final irony is provided by the boy in question, when he transfers his loyalty from his dishonored father to the superficially virtuous coach and athlete. Though this piece contains the characteristic ironic distance, conversational style, and sinister overtones of *Esquire* fiction, the ironies here are too forced and the sub-plots too tangled for this to be considered really effective work.

By the end of 1936, *Esquire* had undergone a few changes, most of which did nothing to alter its basic format. The one that had the most significant effect was the increase in the magazine's size to more than two hundred pages, permitting the publication of pieces longer than the earlier two or three thousand words per story. Noteworthy, but ultimately less important, were changes in writing personnel. In the summer of that year, Hemingway took his leave to cover the Spanish Civil War for *Collier's*, ending his relationship with *Esquire* in a flurry of fiction that included "The Tradesman's Return," a foreshadowing of *To Have and Have Not*, and "The Snows of Kilimanjaro." John Dos Passos stayed on, however, with a series of articles on Spain and the way the war was affecting the people, while composer George Antheil contributed frequent articles on the situation in Nazi Germany. About this time, George Jean Nathan replaced John V. A. Weaver as regular theatre critic.

Increasingly evident in the magazine were stories in the earthy, often grotesque Faulknerian vein of local color, typified by John Steinbeck's "The Lonesome Vigilante," the first-person narrative of a man who is seeking company after participating in a lynching, and his "The Ears of Johnny Bear." Another first-person narrative, this time set in Steinbeck's central California coast, the latter features an ape-like idiot—the Johnny Bear of the title—who can mimic perfectly any conversation he hears. He ends up revealing the sordid inner lives of the community's respected first ladies, one of whom, it turns out, commits suicide because she is pregnant, though unmarried. The final gothic revelation, obvious though left to interference, is that the father of the child was one of the Chinese laborers on the woman's farm estate. Other practitioners of the genre were Erskine Caldwall, Vardis Fisher, and, in its more benign forms, Jesse Stuart, who was to become the most-published contributor to *Esquire* during Gingrich's editorship, the only writer to appear more than Fitzgerald (Gingrich, p. 307).

In general the magazine's fiction continued to swing between sinister, sometimes almost gothic, tales of realistic or naturalistic horror and far subtler stories of the *Smart Set*-style sophistication, sometimes light, sometimes gloomy, but frequently sexual in theme. Typical of the latter is Joseph E. McDougall's "Queen in the Parlor Car," in which a woman endeavors to seduce a willing man, but passes out from intoxication well before consummation. The man, the narrator, remains with her for the night without taking advantage of her. In the morning, he lets her believe they made love; later, she leaves him a note explaining that she had been trying to end her faithful affection for another man, but that now she regretted having done so, ironically yearning for the virtue she had never lost. So ubiquitous were such sexual themes and painful endings that at least one reader, a Princeton freshman, complained in the February 1937 letters-to-the-editor section (called then, as now, "The Sound and the Fury") that the magazine contained entirely too much of both.

All of Fitzgerald's 1937 contributions reflect either the sinister-cum-gothic or the pessimistic-ironic propensities of the periodical, though sexual motifs appear in only one of them. The first story, "An Alcoholic Case" (February), clearly has its roots in Fitzgerald's own wrestle with drink. In it, a private nurse struggles to help a weak-willed commercial artist, a cartoonist, stay dry. Most of the story is taken up with her deciding to keep the case despite the willingness of her agency to assign her elsewhere. When she returns to the alcoholic near the conclusion, it is only to watch him succumb to death. As in so many of his *Esquire* pieces, Fitzgerald maintains a distance that prevents the reader from identifying too closely with any of the characters; the nurse lacks sufficent sophistication, and the alcoholic is perceived only at second hand. Worthy of note is the central presence of medical personnel, a motif of Fitzgerald's last *Post* period, which came to a close the very next month with the publication of "'Trouble.'"

His next piece for *Esquire*, "The Honor of the Goon" (June 1937), opens on a college campus—a setting early associated with Fitzgerald—but quickly moves from the silly to the semi-sinister. The main character is a young man who has perfected the art of taking pratfalls down stairways. The story heads off in another direction, however, after a female foreign student of oriental extraction expresses sincere concern for him after one such performance. The protagonist, embarrassed, initiates the soon spreading practice of calling the woman "the goon." One day an oily oriental man appears and directs his muscular Swedish chauffeur to clout both the college man and his roommate and deface all the photographs of their loved ones. The overall tone of the story wavers, and its point is decidedly unclear. With its careless plotting and hazy point of view, it suffers from an inferiority much resembling the author's work elsewhere at this time.

With "The Long Way Out" (September 1937), however, Fitzgerald returns to quasi-autobiographical material, producing one of his better bits of fiction for *Esquire*. It opens with a first-person narrator discussing oubliettes, then shifts quickly to a story told by a doctor of a young woman in an asylum whose husband was killed just as she was being permitted to go out with him on an outing. When she is finally told the truth, she refuses to believe it and continues contentedly dressing up day after day to meet him. Having finished the tale, which is related by the first narrator in third person, the doctor begs to return to the suddenly less unpleasant subject of oubliettes. Though the connection of the woman's madness with the medieval form of the punishment lends the narrative a mild gothic touch, the metaphor is an apt one. The story succeeds by underplaying and, again, distancing its dramatic material, once more through the vehicle of point of view, *i.e.*, multiple narrators. The story is also terse and to the point. Some readers of the time even noticed this one's superiority; as one regular contributor to "The Sound and the Fury" expressed it: "'The Long Way Out'"...was excellent. It is the first story of his I have ever read that sounded like *true* fiction—the others all sound as if he makes them up...."

His last two stories of 1937 return to the sinister melodrama, however. "The Guest in Room Nineteen" (October) makes use of the old and rare Fitzgerald motif—the mistaking of the real for the supernatural; here an old man dies as a result of his belief that a mysterious boarder in the building where he lives is the personification of death, when in fact he is the landlord's brother. "In the Holidays" (December) is an understated murder melodrama in which the gangster-victim and the colleague who arranges his execution are both concealing themselves in a hospital. In an ironic twist, the reader shares the latter's point of view up to the revelation that he has been responsible for the murder. Though both fit well the standard motifs and techniques of *Esquire*, they are marred by what appears to be hasty writing and a too insistent O. Henry-like irony.

One more story concluded this sequence in January 1938, and it shows Fitzgerald returning once more to autobiographical material. "Financing Finnegan" had, since mid-1937, been sent to a number of Fitzgerald's better-paying former markets, the *Post* and the *American* among them, and been rejected by all before Fitzgerald decided to send it to Gingrich as partial return on the editor's advances. Perhaps ironically, the story itself is rooted in Fitzgerald's dependence on his agent and his editors (Perkins and Gingrich) for funds. Finnegan is a periodically popular, highly creative, but forever indebted author about whom the first-person narrator, a writer himself, states:

> His was indeed a name with ingots in it. His career had started brilliantly and if it had not kept up to its first exhalted level, at least it started brilliantly all over again every few years. He was the perennial

man of promise in American letters—what he could actually do with words was astounding, they glowed and corruscated—he wrote sentences, paragraphs, chapters that were masterpieces of fine weaving and spinning.

This modest evaluation applies to a character who is in other respects decidedly Fitzgerald-like, although one critic has recently suggested some intriguing analogies with Hemingway (George Monteiro, "Two Sets of Books, One Balance Sheet: 'Financing Finnegan,'" in *The Short Stories of F. Scott Fitzgerald*, cited above, p. 291-99). Most like Fitzgerald is the focal character's heavy, perpetual monetary indebtedness to the people who surround him professionally. The narrator relays with some bemusement the repeated assurances from the creditor agent and editor regarding the imminent rebirth of Finnegan's success.

Finnegan appears to have paid them back when he disappears in the Arctic after making them the beneficiaries of his life insurance policy. The prodigal turns up again, however, to the qualified relief of all. In a final touch, the narrator lends two hundred dollars to get Finnegan back to the States and ends up, unrepaid, defending Finnegan's reputation in terms reminiscent of the other creditors. Despite the improbable plot device of sending the writer to the North Pole in search of material, this story bears marks of Fitzgerald's better work for the magazine, particularly the subtlety of the irony and the objectivity produced through the use of a first-person narrator and layered points of view. Though this story was not written specifically for *Esquire*, it shows how the magazine's aesthetics had come to dominate Fitzgerald's artistry.

Besides his *Esquire* fiction and his last story in the *Post*, Fitzgerald placed three minor pieces elsewhere in 1937, two in *The New Yorker*—"Obit on Parnassus," a short poem appearing June 5, and "A Book of One's Own," a humorous article published August 21—and an essay "Early Success" in the October *American Cavalcade*. By the January 1938 appearance of "Financing Finnegan," Fitzgerald was well ensconced in Hollywood, earning a comfortable living as an MGM scriptwriter. Nearly two years would pass before he turned up in the popular press again. Then, from November 1939 to July 1941, Fitzgerald would appear every month in *Esquire*. The only other stories of his to be published in this period were three from an earlier phase: "Strange Sanctuary," the rewritten Gwen story that appeared in the 9 December 1939 issue of *Liberty*, the oft-rejected "The End of Hate," finally printed in the 22 June 1940 *Collier's*, and "Gods of Darkness," the last installation of the Philippe series, held back by *Redbook* until November 1941—eleven months after Fitzgerald's premature death in December 1940.

Considering that Fitzgerald had been immersed in the world of Hollywood since July 1937, it is not surprising that Hollywood dominated the fiction of his last years. Not only did he produce the unfinished novel *The Last Tycoon*, but the majority of his stories for *Esquire* belonged to the Pat Hobby series, which features a conniving but pathetic "scenario hack" struggling for survival in the back lot jungle of Hollywood. It looked as though Fitzgerald had finally found a new and relatively unexploited (by him) source of material. Before the onset of Pat Hobby, however, Fitzgerald published two other stories in *Esquire*, both also reflecting autobiographical material.

"Design in Plaster," published November 1939, found itself in a magazine only slightly changed from the *Esquire* of the mid-thirties. Most noticeable were alterations in print style and lay-out, a surprising new modesty in cartoon illustrations, and the preponderance of the European war in the non-fiction department. Sports and men's fashion continued prominent, as did humor, particularly sexual humor, and stories with racy, pessimistic, and ironic touches. Fitzgerald's story has all three of the latter: a man who has broken his shoulder—just as Fitzgerald once had, diving into a swimming pool—worries about his estranged wife's socializing with a married Frenchman. Jealously endeavoring to keep them apart, the man struggles to his wife's door, where he falls and re-breaks his shoulder. After getting him back to the hospital, the wife, suddenly in need of comfort, calls the Frenchman to her. The story ends with her asking him to her bedroom. The protagonist, ironically, has precipitated the very situation he was trying to prevent. Whatever else may be said of this story, it is good, mainstream *Esquire* fiction.

"The Lost Decade," published the following month, is very short, probably less than two thousand words. It is related in third person from the point of view of a newspaperman who has been given the task of escorting a visitor around the city, a man who has apparently been gone for a decade. The reporter only realizes at the end of the afternoon that the man has been intoxicated for ten years and is only now becoming reacquainted with the world (although James L. W. West, in the article cited above, offers another novel, if not quite convincing, interpretation of the story). This subtle tale, free of melodrama and obvious plot tricks, is one of Fitzgerald's more tightly crafted and artistically effective pieces, even for *Esquire*, and as such merits attention and indeed praise.

The Pat Hobby series began the next month, January 1940, with "Pat Hobby's Christmas Wish," and would run through seventeen installments in as many consecutive months through May 1941. In order of appearance, the others are "A Man in the Way," "'Boil Some Water—Lots of It,'" "Teamed With Genius," "Pat Hobby and Orson Welles," "Pat Hobby's Secret," "Pat Hobby, Putative Father," "The Homes of the Stars," "Pat Hobby Does His Bit," "Pat Hobby's Preview," "No Harm Trying," "A Patriotic Short," "On the Trail of Pat Hobby," "Fun in an Artist's Studio," "Two Old-Timers," "Mightier Than the Sword," and "Pat Hobby's College Days." They all concern the tribulations of a has-been screenwriter, now out of favor, perpetually broke and drunk and willing to do anything to get or remain on the payroll for one more week. In most of them, Pat Hobby—always forty-nine and red-eyed—is lying, cheating, or finagling his way into a writing job or a screen credit, only to have his fraudulent behavior exposed at the end.

A representative tale in this vein is "Teamed with Genius," in which the writer is given the task of working with a well-known English playwright on a screen script. He is unable to get the playwright to work during the day and decides to do the script by himself, looking forward to full screen credit. He is therefore horrified when the playwright comes in one morning with a complete script he has been working on alone at night. Desperate, he gets the playwright out of the way on a pretext, has a secretary steal what he believes to be the script, changes a few lines, and submits it as their collaboration. It turns out that the secretary is the playwright's girlfriend and that the script she gave him was the version that had been rejected a year before.

Though this story and others like it make use of the "trickster tricked" motif, Hobby is not made to look villainous; instead, his acts are the result of "the precarious balance and the sad compromises to which man is exposed in his daily struggle...where life is dominated by the rules of economic power" (Perosa, p. 149). In some sense, Hobby is an existentialist anti-hero: constantly struggling for bare survival with failure forever tripping him, enduring the sundry minor tragedies of existence by pursuing his craft like some parody of a Hemingway protagonist, without the latter's steely dignity.

On the whole, the author-narrator's attitude toward Hobby—indeed, toward all the characters—is one of tolerant, slightly superior bemusement, bordering on but never quite slipping into ridicule. Only once in the series is the reader permitted to feel real pity for Hobby, in "A Patriotic Short," the story that comes the closest to standing on its own merits. In it, Pat is assigned to do a short film about a nineteenth-century military hero on behalf of the World War II effort. Throughout the day his mind slides from studio work to an incident in his more successful past, when the President visited him at his own swimming pool. The brutal contrast between the rosy past and the seedy present recurs in jarring juxtapositions of passages in the narrative. For instance:

> The executives of the company were all dressed up—from a window of his long lost Beverly Hills house Pat had seen Mr. Maranda, whose mansion was next door to him, bustle down his walk in a cutaway coat at nine o'clock, and had known that something was up. He thought maybe it was clergy but when he reached the lot he had found it was the President of the United States himself who was coming...
> "Clean up the stuff about Spain," Ben Brown was saying. "The guy that wrote it was a Red and he's got all the Spanish officers with ants in their pants. Fix up that."

At the end of the story, which as a whole is much less plotted than the others, Pat is nearly run over in a corridor by two studio superiors escorting the starlet of the hour. He returns to his office where, in pathetic protest, he writes an angrily rebellious line that no one will ever see, after which, "he bent down over his desk, his shoulders shaking as he thought of that happy day when he had had a swimming pool." The other sixteen installments lack such effective touches.

The consensus among critics seems clear that either individually or in toto the Pat Hobby stories are minor achievements (see, for instance, Perosa, p. 150; Eble, p. 143; Higgins, p. 177). Their greatest distinction lies in the matter of craft: in the economy and objectivity of Fitzgerald's manner and in the carefully constructed, if repetitive, plots. In these stories the author has "renounced the ornate word for the effective one, turned the musical sentences into terse and direct statements, reduced the full narration to the scantiness of effects of a movie script" (Perosa, p. 151). The author-narrator embodies the distant, ironic, uninvolved stance that Fitzgerald had been practicing throughout his *Esquire* fiction. A good example of this narrative approach is the opening paragraph of "Pat Hobby's Secret":

> Distress in Hollywood is endemic and always acute. Scarcely an executive but is always being gnawed at by some insoluble problem and in a democratic way he will let you in on it, with no charge. The problem, be it one of health or of production, is faced courageously and with groans at from one to five thousand a week. That's how pictures are made.

The sentences are short, and not only is the romance and glitter of Hollywood wholly absent, so is that of the early Fitzgerald. On the other hand, the irony present is anything but ponderous.

Another aspect of the Pat Hobby stories frequently noted by critics is the possible relationship of the protagonist to Fitzgerald's own self-image. Certain parallels between author and character are obvious: Hobby like Fitzgerald has problems with debt and alcohol; like many a Fitzgeraldian hero he is forced to compare his glorious past to his bleak present (Hobby had earned $3,000 per week as a screenwriter in the twenties—Fitzgerald's average story price at the *Post*—contrasted with the $250 per week he can draw now—Fitzgerald's top *Esquire* price). Indeed, Hobby's gestation must have begun around the time of "The Crack-Up"; characteristics of the hack-to-be are evident in the cynical final portion of "Handle With Care." Hobby himself, were he literate enough, could have written the following:

> If you are young and you should write asking to see me and learn how to be a sombre literary man...if you should be so young and so fatuous as to do this, I would not do so much as acknowledge your letter, unless you were related to someone very rich and important indeed. And if you were dying of starvation outside my window, I would go out quickly and give you a smile and the voice (if no longer a hand) and stick around till somebody raised a nickel to phone for the ambulance, that is if I thought there would be any copy in it for me.

"I have now at last become a writer only," reads the next line, but this assertion is not the renewed commitment to his art some have taken it to be. Pat Hobby is "a writer only," as he himself indicates at the end of "Mightier Than the Sword," when he says of the Hollywood establishment, "They don't want authors. They want writers—like me." An author is a person who produces literature; a writer is a man who scribbles for money, who, to paraphrase Gingrich regarding Fitzgerald, writes for a living rather than living for his work (Gingrich, p. 287). Gingrich must have had some awareness of Fitzgerald's attitude toward his work for *Esquire*, which the author called "unprofitable hacking" in a letter to Maxwell Perkins written in the midst of the Hobby series (*Letters*, p. 286). Nevertheless, Fitzgerald devoted much attention to revising these stories, as Gingrich recounts in his introduction to the collected *The Pat Hobby Stories* (New York: Scribner's, 1962). They cannot be considered fine art, but they do demonstrate a competence in craft manifested in too little of Fitzgerald's work of the late thirties. They stand as a testament to Fitzgerald's renewed vigor as a producer of popular fiction.

Only three other stories by Fitzgerald appeared in *Esquire* within the range of his career, printed posthumously during and after the last Pat Hobby pieces in 1941. Gingrich marks that year as the one when *Esquire* pulled away from its early literary phase, which ended in his mind with the death of Fitzgerald (Gingrich, p. 289). The January 1941 number carries almost none of the famous names of previous years; only Nathan, still doing theatre reviews, and Fitzgerald, appearing here with "On the Trail of Pat Hobby," remain of the group that had included Hemingway, Dreiser, Dos Passos, and Pound. On the other hand, this issue contains something by almost everyone of the periodical's then current stable, represented in the fiction department by Manuel Komroff with a piece concerning the Biblical Pilate and Herod, Erskine Caldwell with "Squire Dinwiddy," about a droll but suspicious black who comes to work for a couple living in rural Connecticut, Paul Gallico with a boxing farce, Jesse Stuart with more benign Kentucky local color, Sandor Hunyady with a tale of a lusty Armenian who dies of living too well and whose family celebrates his wake in kind, and Louis Zara with a humorous vernacular yarn about the remarriage of the first-person narrator's aged "pa."

The lead story, Irwin Shaw's "The Eighty-Yard Run," treats a theme dear to Fitzgerald. It opens with a man's recollection of the greatest moment of his life: his making an eighty-yard run during a college football practice—the same day his girlfriend yields herself to him. From then on, however, his life slides downhill. While on the team he never does anything as spectacular in an actual game; he graduates, marries the girl, and enters her father's business, which crumbles with the Crash. While the ex-star turns to drink, his wife begins a career in the intellectual realm of magazine publication, and they grow further apart. He finally gets a job as a campus representative for a men's clothier; it is while visiting his old campus that these recollections have taken place. Somewhat pathetically, he reruns his old moment of glory on the field.

Of all the stories in this issue, Shaw's comes the closest to the ethos of the original *Esquire*, with subtle effects, a melancholy message, irony, and a hint of eroticism. The other fiction from regulars leans heavily on character types and local color, very much like material prominent in *The American Mercury* a decade earlier, though on the whole lighter. Unchanged is the preponderance of sports features, though now crowded by articles on the war. The modesty that had crept into the cartoons was more than made up for by the new two-page illustrations of nude or scantily clad women by Petty and Vargas. Ironically, American entry into the war at the end of the year would accelerate the above trends, producing more wholesome, positive reading matter even as the pin-ups became larger and sexier—both in the interests of troop "morale."

Fitzgerald's fiction, however, firmly pursued its own course, in large part because his last non-Hobby stories had been written as much as a year or so before, but had been held back until the series was finished. Frustrated by *Esquire*'s low rates and desperate for money that would allow him to work on his novel, Fitzgerald insisted that Gingrich publish these stories alongside Hobby under a pseudonym, so as not to violate Gingrich's editorial policy mandating no more than one piece per author per issue. This was the primary reason for the appearance of "On an Ocean Wave" under the pen name Paul Elgin in the February 1941 number, and not, as some have implied, because the author was "tired of being Scott Fitzgerald" (*Letters*, p. 599; quoted by Piper, p. 255), which was an afterthought.

"On an Ocean Wave" harks back to the sinister manner of "The Guest in Room Nineteen" and "In the Holidays." It features a powerful capitalist who is taking a sea cruise with both his wife and mistress in attendance. When a traveling college professor takes an interest in the much-neglected wife, the capitalist has the man thrown overboard to his death. The tale ends sardonically with the unsuspecting wife breathlessly awaiting her assignation. Like the other two stories, it is among his less interesting; plot, point of view, and style all lack focus, and while relatively un-melodramatic the story possesses, like the earlier ones, a too insistent irony.

In "The Woman from Twenty-One," published in June, Fitzgerald is in more familiar territory. In this short episode, a man who has returned to New York with his Eurasian wife after a long absence in Java finds himself adjacent to an obnoxious, intoxicated, wealthy woman of thirty-five in a Broadway theatre. As she begs her companions to take her back to the Club Twenty-One, he notices that she seems to be an old flame of his. Her behavior worsens, and shortly before her party leaves the theatre the man sees in her all the reasons he originally left New York. The story is subtle, so subtle, in fact, as to be confusing on the first reading, but at least it avoids the stagey effects of pieces like the previous one.

The most successful story of the last group is "Three Hours Between Planes," issued in July as the last *Esquire* story published during his career. Donald Plant, attempting to fill the interval between plane connections, looks up a woman who had once snubbed him before either of them had reached adolescence. He finds her married but temporarily alone and thrilled to see him. They exchange reminiscences, then a prolonged kiss, and he wonders what sort of woman she has been. He learns when she brings out an old photograph album and he discovers she has confused him with another male in her past. Turning suddenly chilly, she sends him away. The story concludes with the line: "Donald had lost a good deal too in those hours between planes—but since the second half of life is a long process of getting rid of things, that part of the experience probably didn't matter." While "Between Planes" echoes the old Fitzgerald theme of trying unsuccessfully to relive the past, it ends on a more resigned and realistic note than, say, "Winter Dreams."

Though Gingrich was quite broad-minded in his acceptance of Fitzgerald's fiction, as the diversity in theme and quality of the 1941 stories alone demonstrates, it merits noting that not everything the author sent in was purchased, particularly near the end of his *Esquire* period. One story returned was "Dearly Beloved," a short piece, well under one thousand words, which summarizes the pathetic adult lives of a black man, a porter who reads Plato and longs to be a golf champion, and his simple, loving wife. In style the sketch swings from the apos-

The Price of Paradise

trophic ("O Beauty Boy—reading Plato so divine! O dark, oh fair, colored golf champion of Chicago") to the colloquial ("So things go"), running through the various mishaps sustained by the couple with no dialogue and no sense of involvement or immediacy whatsoever. Eventually both man and wife die of influenza and go to heaven, where he finally reaches his dream of becoming golf champion. "Dearly Beloved" must be regarded either as an experiment that failed or as a hasty grab at another $250 of emergency money too blatantly careless even for Gingrich.

There can be little question that the work Fitzgerald published in *Esquire* is markedly different in a number of ways from the fiction which characterized the rest of his magazine career. For Higgins, the contrast between his relatively sparse *Esquire* stories and the romances he was writing in the thirties for other magazines "proves that Fitzgerald did make a practice of altering his style, when necessary, to sell a story to a particular magazine" (p. 183). "The effect of his switch to *Esquire* was considerable on his subject matter," Higgins states elsewhere, "but far greater on his technique" (p. 149). Perosa more cautiously detects the influence of *Esquire* on Fitzgerald's manner, observing that the author's new style of the late thirties, which emphasized brevity, compression, and essentiality,

> was perhaps determined—if only marginally—by the fact that most of these stories and sketches were written for the magazine *Esquire* and were therefore conditioned from the very start by the limited number of pages available and by the comparatively small amount of money that Fitzgerald received for them.

He goes on to insist, however, that by and large "Fitzgerald found his new 'measure' by himself and did not submit to any particular requirements of the magazine" (p. 147). He uses as evidence *The Last Tycoon*, which Fitzgerald had begun composing late in 1939 about the time he had finished the first Pat Hobby stories. The unfinished novel possesses, according to Perosa, "a quite different type of diction—a diction which came as close as possible to the ideal of immediacy and concreteness that is present in Hemingway's fiction" (p. 152), and he writes that this "bare, unadorned style [was] perfectly in keeping with the crude reality it had to express" (p. 167).

If Perosa divorces what he sees as the compression of *The Last Tycoon* from the influence of *Esquire*, Hindus goes further, regarding *Tycoon*'s effects as a reflection of neither Hemingway nor *Esquire*, but of Hollywood scenario writing (p. 72). Other critics do not even view the novel's technique as all that compressed, thus removing it to an even greater distance from Fitzgerald's work for the magazine. Eble, for instance, maintains that in its later stages the novel was slipping toward the all-inclusive, elaborative manner of *Tender Is the Night*, despite Fitzgerald's original intention to write *The Last Tycoon* "as a *constructed* novel like *Gatsby*, with passages of poetic prose when it fits the action" (*Letters*, p. 128). The discussion of the *The Last Tycoon* is pertinent here because Fitzgerald's novels always represented what he considered his "serious" work; the absence of clear parallels in technique between this novel and his *Esquire* fiction would suggest that the latter was written less to artistic than to periodical parameters, or at least that he did not regard it in the mainstream of his development.

On the other hand, Fitzgerald was using elements of his *Esquire* style well before the magazine's conception. The brevity and compression characteristic of his *Esquire* pieces is evident, for instance, in his "Outside the Cabinet-Maker's," published in 1928 in *Century*, while it is the Hemingwayesque terseness of the dialogue at the climax of "The Rich Boy" of 1926 that contributes so much to the story's effectiveness. The reason he did not continue to use such techniques regularly, according to Higgins, was that "the conventional stylistic requirements of the *Post* and other big-money magazines...kept Fitzgerald from further use of his other style until he began writing for *Esquire*" (p. 159). Fitzgerald did keep himself fairly close to his early romantic manner for the most part of his career, even when inspiration flagged; it was what most editors had come to expect from him and what by and large he expected of himself. One properly concludes that *Esquire* did not create his stripped style, but that its editorial requirements and preferences merely permitted, or at most encouraged, Fitzgerald to practice it.

The same can be said for other aspects of his *Esquire* technique. Concerning point of view, for instance, Fitzgerald pretty much abandoned in *Esquire* the self-conscious authorial voice of much of his earlier work—the friendly reader's guide of the *Post* and its imitators, and the cynical and bemused narrator of *The Smart Set*. The third-person author-narrator of the *Esquire* fiction is far removed from the activity of the plot and virtually never comments upon it. Even where the narrator speaks in first person, he/she often either is too naive to court identification with the reader, as in "The Night before Chancellorsville," or merely provides a frame for another party's narration, as in "'I Didn't Get Over'" and "The Long Way Out." Effective methods of establishing objective distance between reader and characters, they were not new to Fitzgerald either; the most notable example of earlier use is Jordan Baker's third-person narration of Gatsby's past within the frame of Nick Carraway's tale.

Thematically, Fitzgerald took the opportunity provided him by Gingrich's indulgence to range far from his traditional romantic material, though this opportunity led him oft astray into melodrama—"The Fiend," "On an Ocean Wave," etc.—and onto other more unfortunate paths which ended in such O. Henry-like products as "The Guest in Room Nineteen" and "In the Holidays" and in the downright silly "Shaggy's Morning," "The Ants of Princeton," and "The Honor of the Goon."

Perhaps logically, his *Esquire* pieces that most interest critics are those that lean to the autobiographical: the "Crack-Up" and "Author" series, as well as the more fictionalized "An Alcoholic Case," "The Long Way Out," "Financing Finnegan," "Design in Plaster," and "The Lost Decade." It is in these, along with the archetypically Fitzgeraldian "Three Hour Between Planes," that the author's experiments with point of view seem to work out best, for here material full of significance and emotional coloring for Fitzgerald is objectified, regarded with the distant, subtly ironic eye of the modern artist. Here Fitzgerald comes closest to reducing all he holds valuable to quintessential pearls of great price, in contrast to his tendency widely evident elsewhere—particularly in his *Post* pieces but even in something as slight as "Dearly Beloved"—of stretching his matter out as thinly as possible and padding it with rhetoric, transparent plot devices, and twist endings.

Between his best and his worst for *Esquire* stands a substantial body of fiction demonstrating the competence of the professional writer *sans* the marks of the artist, a group embracing all the Pat Hobby stories, "The Night Before Chancellorsville," "'I Didn't Get Over,'" and little else. Considering that Gingrich gave Fitzgerald free rein over his pen, one must conclude from the mediocrity of much of the author's work either that Fitzgerald thought little of the magazine as a market or that he had indeed become "a writer only." The evidence of his correspondence (recall the above-quoted remark to Perkins about his *Esquire* work being "unprofitable hacking") and of his concurrent work in Hollywood suggests a measure of both possibilities.

There can be little doubt that *Esquire* offered Fitzgerald a chance to experiment with new forms and methods and to polish those that had worked best for him in the past, independent of the constraints of the general audience periodicals and of the themes and manners associated with his reputation—a chance he had often expressed a desire for in earlier stages of his career. Good or bad, his work for *Esquire* is distinct from the majority of his writing elsewhere. However, when one weighs the rich, poignant bathos of "The Crack-Up" against the proficient but ultimately redundant craft of the Pat Hobby stories, one can only conclude that Fitzgerald was unwilling or unable to take advantage of this opportunity to exercise his art to its fullest extent and produce a truly superior body of work.

VI.

THE END OF A LIFE, THE BEGINNING OF A LEGEND

The obituary essays and editorials that came out in the wake of Fitzgerald's death by heart attack on 21 December 1940 ranged from the supercilious to the laudatory. The majority of them, however, found it difficult to get past the early works that had made his reputation. As Arnold Gingrich noted in an *Esquire* editorial,

> [E]verybody seemed bent on remembering him for his worst book, *Flappers and Philosophers*, and forgetting all about the book by which he will be remembered. In most of the newspaper stories *The Great Gatsby* was given mere passing mention, if any at all, while most of the space was devoted to *This Side of Paradise*....In general, the American press dismissed the death of the author of *The Great Gatsby* as if he were merely a sort of verbal counterpart of John Held, Jr. ("Salute and Farewell to F. Scott Fitzgerald," March 1941, p. 6)

Yet even Gingrich observed in the same place that "it is doubtful that more than one novel and a handful of short stories will endure, out of Scott Fitzgerald's many writings over the past twenty years."

When one reviews the whole of Fitzgerald's professional career, perhaps it should not be surprising, if lamentable, that his later novels were swallowed up by his popular reputation. Since *This Side of Paradise*, he had sustained his contact with the public—not to mention again his livelihood—via the more than 170 short pieces he sold to wide-circulation periodicals. Most of these traded quite lucratively on

Fitzgerald's notoriety as spokesman or ex-spokesman for youth, modern romance, and the Jazz Age.

In the decade following his death, a number of Fitzgerald's friends and colleagues worked hard to redeem his critical standing from the dust-bin. Edmund Wilson must be credited with much of the impetus of the Fitzgerald revival, with his 1941 edition of *The Last Tycoon* and his 1945 collection, *The Crack-Up*. The first major effort toward serious criticism was the collection of essays, *F. Scott Fitzgerald: The Man and His Work*, edited by Alfred Kazin and published in 1951, the year that also saw the appearance of Arthur Mizener's biography and Malcolm Cowley's edition of twenty-eight short stories. That these early endeavors succeeded in bringing Fitzgerald to the attention of serious critics is now a matter of record.

In the process, however, as noted earlier, scholars have embraced the novels and the best short works while largely neglecting the major portion of this author's canon. In some respects, these critics, by considering only Fitzgerald's "serious" work, have erred as much in one direction as Fitzgerald's unthinking detractors did in the other at the time of his death. When faced with the sheer volume of the product of the author's twenty-year writing career, it is difficult to imagine how any balanced assessment of his artistry and significance can be made while ignoring so large a part of his total work and the part to which he devoted the greatest number of years.

Let us briefly review this body of work from the standpoint of this study. Fitzgerald was introduced to the reading public in 1919 via *The Smart Set* of H. L. Mencken and George Jean Nathan. He already shared with this periodical and its editors roots in the British aesthetic movement of the 1890s, and he learned through Mencken about the American naturalism of the same decade. Fitzgerald retained his identification with the cynical gaiety, the superficial pessimism, and the aristocratic *hauteur* of *The Smart Set* for some years, aided by his reputation of ostensible disillusionment and rebellion against accepted mores derived from the notoriety of *This Side of Paradise*. A number of motifs associated with the early Fitzgerald—the fascination with the rich and/or aristocratic, the epigrammatic cleverness, the sly romantic adventurism, and even the distaste for age and aging—were all already part of *The Smart Set* ethos before Fitzgerald arrived. While this relationship places Fitzgerald closer to the avant-garde of the previous generation than to his own postwar coevals—e.e. cummings, John Dos Passos, and Hemingway—it gives him an aura of continuity with the

The Price of Paradise

American cultural past that the others lack. This same continuity is noted repeatedly by Austin McGiffert Wright in *The American Short Story in the Twenties*, cited above.

Fitzgerald's proximity to the mainstream of American thought is more apparent in his long association with *The Saturday Evening Post*. Here his reputed rebelliousness and high spirits mingled with the romantic individualism of the middle-class. As was pointed out earlier, and as Robert Sklar observes throughout his study *The Last Laocoon*, no real conflict exists between Fitzgerald's essential idealism, melancholy though it sometimes seems, and the optimistic urge for success, wealth, and romance so characteristic of the American mind and of Lorimer's magazine; in fact, "in his own person he was acting out the role of the genteel tradition's romantic hero" (Sklar, p. 5). Several of Fitzgerald's better stories were written for the *Post*—indeed, some of his best—and the charge that the *Post*'s standards ruined his artistic career seems, upon analysis, less credible than the idea that Fitzgerald exhausted his imagination trying to keep himself on the magazine's payroll.

This last contention is borne out by the work he produced for other magazines, particularly as the thirties wore on. While in the twenties an occasional masterpiece like "The Rich Boy" had offset the general run of mediocre stories, no such bright spots appear in his fiction for the same periodicals a decade later. He came close to repeating his successes on different terms in some of his fiction for the men's magazine *Esquire*, though the autobiographical essays he did for this journal overshadow the fiction. And in the case of *Esquire*, the author and his apologists do not have editorial strictures to blame; Gingrich was a passionate admirer of Fitzgerald's work and invited him to submit anything he wanted to write. Although Fitzgerald did take this opportunity to pull away from the stories of young love that had come to be expected of him, most of the result unfortunately merits little serious attention. The most significant difference between his work for *Esquire* and that for other magazines is technical: Fitzgerald made use of the space limitations and low pay of the former to experiment with the stripped style, the restricted point of view, and the dramatic, detached narrator, techniques he had utilized before, albeit rarely.

What, ultimately, does this analysis of the periodicals and Fitzgerald's work for them add to his critical reputation? For one thing, it tends to undermine certain critical clichés perpetuating the belief that Fitzgerald was artistically hamstrung by the editors for which he wrote;

the occasional necessity for compromise was nowhere near as debilitating to Fitzgerald's craft as other, more personal factors. Perhaps the biggest problem in his short fiction, though not restricted to it, is his difficulty with plotting. A number of critics are now willing to admit that Fitzgerald was inherently weak when it came to plots. Hindus expresses the issue thus:

> Of his novels, four out of five are deficient in some points of construction. Their plots not only lack clarity but are at times positively obscure or confused....It might appear, at first thought, that the briefer compass of his short stories would make it easier for Fitzgerald to achieve the clarity and unity of construction that he so often missed or spoiled in his longer, more ambitious efforts. But it turns out, upon studying his works, that achieving an artistic unity and compactness is no easier on a small scale than on a large one. (p. 94)

This view is seconded by Bruccoli, Cowley, and Piper, and it is certainly reinforced by much of Fitzgerald's magazine fiction.

For Hindus as for Perosa and others, Fitzgerald's worth lies primarily in the poetry of his style. It was more than style alone, however, that kept him publishable in general interest periodicals throughout his career or that has sustained popular or critical interest in him since his death. There were plenty of competent and even remarkable stylists who shared with him the pages of *The Smart Set*, the *Post* and *Redbook*, writers like James Branch Cabell, Joseph Hergesheimer, and Ben Hecht, none of whom are taken as seriously today. It takes more than poetry to perpetuate a legend.

Nor does Fitzgerald's magazine work make him appear a particularly original or innovative thinker; quite the contrary, it demonstrates how much he belonged to his era—from the Ivy League smartness and disillusionment of the postwar period through the jazzy romanticism of the twenties to the despair of the late Depression. This philosophical consonance with his age matched "his fatal ability to synchronize his most private fortunes and misfortunes with the pattern of each decade he wrote in" (Kazin, from the Introduction to *F. Scott Fitzgerald: The Man and His Work*, Cleveland: World, 1951, p. 16). "[T]hat he was so completely of his time and of his country" was viewed, in the wake of his somewhat demeaning obituaries, as "[h]is greatest weakness" (Charles Weir, Jr., in Kazin, p. 134). Perhaps now we can regard this characteristic as one of his greatest strengths.

Bernard De Voto was squinting in the direction of the truth when he insisted in a *Post* article that future historians would glean the genuine spirit of the age, the texture of the average American life, and the mind of the majority from the slick magazines and not from the highbrow literary organs. Fortunately, in Fitzgerald we have a writer who came from the slicks with enough literary merit to make most of his work readable generations later. More accessible than Faulkner, more varied than Hemingway, he continues to resonate in the popular consciousness decades after his death. Those commentators in the mainstream of Fitzgerald criticism who regard the author as a first-class artist who perennially prostituted his talent in hack work may be taking Fitzgerald and his own self-criticism too seriously. It would be far more fair—indeed, reasonable, judging from the facts of his career—to view him primarily as a prolific popular writer and a characteristic American of his time, who hit a literary zenith with *The Great Gatsby* and rose elsewhere on occasion to remarkable heights, but who, in the bulk of his fiction and non-fiction passed on to later generations a complete psychological portrait of his era.

ABOUT THE AUTHOR

STEPHEN W. POTTS received his Ph.D. in English from the University of California, Berkeley in 1980, after which he spent one year as a Fulbright Fellow teaching American literature in Germany. That year also saw the publication of his first scholarly article (on Stanislaw Lem) and his first fiction sale (to Robert Silverberg's science fiction anthology *New Dimensions 10*). He has since published two monographs on Joseph Heller—including *From Here to Absurdity: The Moral Battlefields of Joseph Heller*, Volume 36 in The Borgo Press's THE MILFORD SERIES: POPULAR WRITERS OF TODAY—as well as articles on F. Scott Fitzgerald, J. R. R. Tolkien, and a number of other American, British, and Slavic authors.

He currently teaches courses in literature, science fiction, fantasy, and popular culture at the University of California, San Diego. While simultaneously marketing a novel through literary agent Richard Curtis, Potts is also working on an updated and revised edition of *From Here to Absurdity*. This is his third book published by The Borgo Press, the most recent being *The Second Marxian Invasion: The Fiction of the Strugatsky Brothers* (1991), a critical analysis of two of Russia's most popular writers, which won the J. Lloyd Eaton Memorial Award for Best Critical Work of the Year.

BIBLIOGRAPHY

I. Primary Bibliography

Afternoon of an Author: A Selection of Uncollected Stories and Essays. Edited, with Introduction, by Arthur Mizener. Princeton: Princeton University Library Press, 1957.

All the Sad Young Men. New York: Scribner's, 1926.

The Apprentice Fiction of F. Scott Fitzgerald, 1909-1917. Edited, with Introduction, by John Kuehl. New Brunswick, NJ: Rutgers University Press, 1965.

As Ever, Scott Fitz—: Letters Between F. Scott Fitzgerald and His Literary Agent Harold Ober, 1919-1940. Edited by Matthew J. Bruccoli, with Jennifer McCabe Atkinson. Preface by Scottie Fitzgerald Smith. Philadelphia: Lippincott, 1972.

Babylon Revisited and Other Stories. New York: Scribner's, 1960.

The Basil and Josephine Stories. Edited, with Introduction, by Jackson R. Bryer and John Kuehl. New York: Scribner's, 1973.

The Beautiful and Damned. New York: Scribner's, 1922.

Bits of Paradise: 21 Uncollected Stories by F. Scott and Zelda Fitzgerald. Edited by Matthew J. Bruccoli, with Scottie Fitzgerald Smith. New York: Scribner's, 1973; New York: Pocket Books, 1976.

The Crack-Up. Edited by Edmund Wilson. New York: New Directions, 1945.

Dear Scott/Dear Max: The Fitzgerald-Perkins Correspondence. Edited by John Kuehl and Jackson R. Bryer. New York: Scribner's, 1971.

F. Scott Fitzgerald: In His Own Time. Edited by Matthew J. Bruccoli and Jackson R. Bryer. New York: Popular Library, 1971.

F. Scott Fitzgerald's Ledger: A Facsimile. Edited, with Introduction, by Mathew J. Bruccoli. Washington, DC: NCR/Microcards, 1972.

The Fitzgerald Reader. Edited by Arthur Mizener. New York: Scribner's, 1963.

Flappers and Philosophers. New York: Scribner's, 1920. With Introduction by Arthur Mizener. New York: Scribner's, 1959.

The Great Gatsby. New York: Scribner's, 1925.

The Last Tycoon. Edited by Edmund Wilson. New York: Scribner's, 1941.
The Letters of F. Scott Fitzgerald. Edited by Andrew Turnbull. New York: Scribner's, 1963.
Letters to His Daughter. Edited by Andrew Turnbull. New York: Scribner's, 1967.
The Notebooks of F. Scott Fitzgerald. Edited by Matthew J. Bruccoli. Bloomfield Hills, MI: Bruccoli Clark, 1978.
The Pat Hobby Stories. Introduction by Arnold Gingrich. New York: Scribner's, 1962.
The Portable F. Scott Fitzgerald. Edited by Dorothy Parker. New York: Viking, 1945.
The Price Was High: The Last Uncollected Stories of F. Scott Fitzgerald. Edited by Matthew J. Bruccoli. New York: Harcourt Brace Jovanovitch, 1979.
Six Tales of the Jazz Age and Other Stories. New York: Scribner's, 1960.
The Stories of F. Scott Fitzgerald. Edited, with Introduction, by Malcolm Cowley. New York: Scribner's, 1951.
Tales of the Jazz Age. New York: Scribner's, 1922.
Taps at Reveille. New York: Scribner's, 1935.
Tender Is the Night. New York: Scribner's, 1934.
This Side of Paradise. New York: Scribner's, 1920.

II. SECONDARY BIBLIOGRAPHY

Atkinson, Jennifer McCabe. "Lost and Unpublished Stories by F. Scott Fitzgerald," in *Fitzgerald/Hemingway Annual*, 1971, p. 32-63.
Bruccoli, Matthew J. *F. Scott Fitzgerald: A Descriptive Bibliography*. Pittsburgh: University of Pittsburgh Press, 1972.
_____. *Some Sort of Epic Grandeur: The Life of F. Scott Fitzgerald*. New York: Harcourt Brace Jovanovitch, 1981.
Bryer, Jackson R. *The Critical Reputation of F. Scott Fitzgerald: A Bibliographical Study*. New Haven: Archon Books, 1967.
_____, ed. *The Short Stories of F. Scott Fitzgerald: New Approaches in Criticism*. Madison, WI: University of Wisconsin Press, 1982.
Cass, Colin. "Fitzgerald's Second Thoughts about *May Day*: A Collation and Study," in *Fitzgerald/Hemingway Annual*, 1970, p. 69-95.
Cowley, Malcolm. *Exile's Return: A Literary Odyssey of the 1920s*. New York: Viking, 1951.
_____. *Fitzgerald and the Jazz Age*. New York: Viking, 1966.
Daniels, Thomas E. "Pat Hobby: Anti-Hero," in *Fitzgerald/Hemingway Annual*, 1973, p. 131-139.
Dolmetsch, Carl R. *The Smart Set: A History and Anthology*. New York: Dial, 1966.

Eble, Kenneth. *F. Scott Fitzgerald, Revised Edition.* Twayne's United States Authors Series. Boston: Twayne, 1977.
_____. "'John Jackson's Arcady' and *The Great Gatsby*," in *Fitzgerald Newsletter* 21 (Spring 1963): 1-2.
Gingrich, Arnold. *Nothing But People: The Early Days at Esquire, A Personal History, 1928-1958.* New York: Crown, 1971.
Goldhurst, William. *F. Scott Fitzgerald and His Contemporaries.* Cleveland: World, 1963.
Higgins, John A. *F. Scott Fitzgerald: A Study of the Stories.* Jamaica, New York: St. John's University Press, 1971.
Hindus, Milton. *F. Scott Fitzgerald: An Introduction and Interpretation.* New York: Holt, Rinehart and Winston, 1968.
Hoffman, Frederick J. *The Twenties: American Writing in the Postwar Decade.* New York: Viking, 1955.
Kazin, Alfred, ed. *F. Scott Fitzgerald: The Man and His Work.* Cleveland: World, 1951.
Lehan, Richard D. *F. Scott Fitzgerald and the Craft of Fiction.* Preface by Harry T. Moore. Carbondale, IL: Southern Illinois University Press, 1966.
Male, Roy R. "'Babylon Revisited': A Story of the Exile's Return," in *Studies in Short Fiction* 2 (Spring 1965): 270-77.
Mencken, H. L. *H. L. Mencken's Smart Set Criticism.* Edited by William H. Nolte. Ithaca, NY: Cornell University Press, 1968.
_____. *The Letters of H. L. Mencken.* Edited by Guy J. Forgue. New York: Knopf, 1961.
_____. *Prejudices: Second Series.* New York: Knopf, 1920.
Miller, James E. *F. Scott Fitzgerald: His Art and Technique.* New York: New York University Press, 1964.
Mizener, Arthur, ed. *F. Scott Fitzgerald: A Collection of Critical Essays.* Englewood Cliffs, NJ: Prentice-Hall, 1963.
_____. *The Far Side of Paradise: A Biography of F. Scott Fitzgerald.* Boston: Houghton Mifflin, 1951.
Nolte, William H. *H. L. Mencken, Literary Critic.* Middletown, CT: Wesleyan University Press, 1966.
Perosa, Sergio. *The Art of F. Scott Fitzgerald.* Ann Arbor, MI: University of Michigan Press, 1965.
Piper, Henry Dan. *F. Scott Fitzgerald: A Critical Portrait.* New York: Holt, Rinehart and Winston, 1965.
Sklar, Robert. *F. Scott Fitzgerald: The Last Laocoon.* New York: Oxford, 1968.
Stevenson, Douglas E. *H. L. Mencken: Iconoclast from Baltimore.* Chicago: University of Chicago Press, 1971.
Tebble, John. *George Horace Lorimer and The Saturday Evening Post.* Garden City, NY: Doubleday, 1948.
Toor, David. "Guilt and Retribution in 'Babylon Revisited,'" in *Fitzgerald/Hemingway Annual*, 1973, p. 155-164.

Turnbull, Andrew. *Scott Fitzgerald*. New York: Scribner's, 1962.
Wilson, Edmund. *The Shores of Light: A Literary Chronicle of the Twenties and Thirties*. New York: Farrar, Straus and Giroux, 1952.
Wood, James Playstead. *Magazines in the United States, Third Edition*. New York: Ronald Press, 1971.
Wright, Austin McGiffert. *The American Short Story in the Twenties*. Chicago: University of Chicago Press, 1961.

INDEX

SUBJECT INDEX

Abdullah, Achmed, 16-17
Adams, Charles Magee, 29
aestheticism, 16, 18-21, 25, 42, 116
Afternoon of an Author, 31
Aiken, Conrad, 86
alcoholism, 9, 24-25, 32, 38, 47, 49, 66-67, 70-72, 77, 88, 92, 101, 107, 113
Alexander, Elizabeth, 59
Alger, Horatio, 61
"*All the Sad Young Men*: Art's Bread and Butter," 53
"*All the Sad Young Men*: The Boy Grows Older," 53
Allen, Hervey—SEE: *Anthony Adverse*
American Booksellers Association, 13
American Cavalcade, 103
The American Magazine, 40, 48, 91, 94, 102
The American Mercury, 43-44, 48, 74, 82, 84-85, 109
The American Short Story in the Twenties, 95, 117
Antheil, George, 100
Anthony Adverse (by Allen), 93
anti-hero, 105
Apparel Arts, 82
"The Art of Bartending," 83
The Art of F. Scott Fitzgerald (by Perosa), 90
Asbury, Herbert, 48
Atkinson, Jennifer McCabe, 10, 94

Atlantic, 31
Atwood, Albert W., 65
Aurelius, Marcus, 23
Austin, F. Britten, 60, 65, 74
author-narrator, 20, 47, 49, 63, 78, 98, 101-102, 108, 113
"Author" series, 97-99, 113
autobiographical material, 31, 60, 77, 83, 86, 89-91, 98, 101-102, 104, 107-108, 113
Balmer, Edwin, 40, 80, 86
Baltimore American, 43
Bartley, Nalbro, 68
Barton, Bruce, 48
Bates, H. E., 85
"Basil Duke Lee" stories, 59-60, 62, 67, 95
"The Bear" (by Faulkner), 93
The Bedside Esquire, 87
Behrman, S. N., 19
"Belasco midnight," 21
Benét, Stephen Vincent, 18
Benét, William Rose, 41, 53
Berlin, Irving, 97
Bierce, Ambrose, 17, 87
Bigger, Earl Derr, 67
Bishop, John Peale, 13
Bits of Paradise (by Bruccoli), 71
"Booboisie," 18
Bookman, 50
Boston Watch and Ward Society, 48
Boyd, Thomas A., 37

Bridges, Robert, 32
Bruccoli, Matthew J., 21, 37, 71, 118
Bryer, Jackson R., 97
"Bull Market" (by Street), 65-66
Bunin, Ivan, 83
Burt, Struthers, 48, 60
"business romance," 15, 27-28, 44-45, 47, 50-51, 56, 59, 61, 65
Butler, Samuel, 23
Cabell, James Branch, 15-16, 118
Caldwell, Erskine, 100, 108
The Call of the Wild, (by London), 15
Callaghan, Morley, 82-84
Campbell, J. L., 85
canine narrator, 88
Cather, Willa, 18, 46
Catholicism, 22, 44
The Century Magazine, 31, 65, 112
Chamberlain, George Agnew, 44, 56-57
Charles Scribner's Sons, 15, 32
"Charlie Chan" (by Bigger), 67
Chesterton, G. K., 13
Chicago Sunday Tribune, 37, 50
Child, Maude Parker, 51
Christie, Agatha, 79, 81
Civil War setting, 87-88, 94
"Climbing" (by van Saanen), 17
Cobb, Irvin S., 40
Cohen, Octavus Roy, 60, 81
College Humor, 49, 65, 74
Collier's, 35, 39, 74, 86, 94, 100, 104
Conrad, Joseph, 15-16, 77
"Coral" (by Hergesheimer), 59
Cosmopolitan, 16, 19, 22, 35, 40, 74, 78, 80, 96

Costain, Thomas B., 55. 64, 92
"The Covered Wagon" (by Hough), 38
Cowley, Malcolm, 95, 116, 118
"Crack-Up" stories, 89-90, 97, 100, 107, 113-114
Crane, Mifflin, 19
Crane, Stephen, 18
cummings, e. e., 116
Cummings, Homer, 85
Curtis Publishing Co., 92
D'Agostino, Guido, 86
Dear Scott/Dear Max, 24, 37, 62, 81, 87
The Decadents, 13
"Defense of Dirty Words" (by Hemingway), 86
Depression, 65-72, 74, 78-80, 82, 92-93, 118
De Voto, Bernard, 15, 65, 67, 95, 119
Dial, 95
Dolmetsch, Carl, 19
Dos Passos, John, 79, 82, 86, 90, 100, 108, 116
Dowson, Ernest Christopher, 16
Doyle, Arthur Conan, 40, 50
Dreiser, Theodore, 15-18, 36, 82-83, 85-86, 90, 108
Dunsany, Lord, 16, 85
"The Ears of Johnny Bear" (by Steinbeck), 100
Eble, Kenneth, 35, 88, 106, 112
"The Eighty-Yard Run" (by Shaw), 108-109
"Elgin, Paul," pseud. of F. Scott Fitzgerald, 109
Ellis, Havelock, 86
epigrammatic style, 20, 116
"Esky," 83
Esquire, 82-90, 97, 99-115, 117

European settings, 71-72
Evarts, Hal G., 60
Exile's Return, 95
"Exit the King" (by Marquis), 63
F. Scott Fitzgerald (by Eble), 35
F. Scott Fitzgerald: A Critical Portrait (by Piper), 19, 31
F. Scott Fitzgerald: A Study of the Stories (by Higgins), 10-11
F. Scott Fitzgerald: An Introduction and Interpretation (by Hindus), 90
F. Scott Fitzgerald: In His Own Time (ed. Bruccoli), 37, 43, 53
F. Scott Fitzgerald: The Man and His Work (ed. Kazin), 116, 118-119
fantasy, 39-40, 79
Faulkner, William 67, 92-93, 100, 119
"Fine Apparel" (by Hergesheimer), 70
Fisher, Vardis, 100
Fitzgerald, Scottie, 88, 91
Fitzgerald, Zelda Sayre, 9, 27, 33, 35, 43, 50, 65, 68-69, 74, 77, 83, 85, 88, 91, 93
"Fitzgerald and *Esquire*" (by West), 97
Fitzgerald/Hemingway Annual, 10, 94
flappers, 14, 21, 24, 27, 29, 36, 41-43, 48, 50, 61, 64, 67-68, 79
"The Folks at Home" (by Hughes), 84
Forgue, Guy J., 17
Gallico, Paul, 108
Garrett, Garet, 65
Gaspar Ruiz (by Conrad), 15

George Horace Lorimer and The Saturday Evening Post (by Tebbel), 14
Gilpatric, Guy, 74
Gingrich, Arnold, 82, 86-90, 97, 100, 102, 108-111, 113, 115, 117
"The Girl who was Easy" (by Callaghan), 83-84
Glass, Montague, 74
Gold, Michael, 79
Gone With the Wind (by Mitchell), 93
"The Gorgeous Girl" (by Bartley), 68
Graeve, Oscar, 56
Graphic, 36
Gray, Davis, 78
"Guide-Posts and Camp-Fires," 31
"Gwen" stories, 91-92, 103
H. L. Mencken: Iconoclast from Baltimore (by Stenerson), 18
Hamilton, Gertrude Brooks, 19
Hansen, Harry, 53
Hapgood, Norman, 40
Harper's Bazaar, 31, 39
Hatteras, Major Owen—SEE: Nathan, George Jean and Mencken, H. L.
Hawthorne, Nathaniel, 87
Hearst's International, 35, 40-42, 46
Hecht, Ben, 18, 25, 86, 118
Held, John, Jr., 50, 115
Hemingway, Ernest, 10, 50, 81-83, 85-86, 90, 100, 103, 105, 108, 111-112, 116, 119
Henry, O., 16, 37, 41, 102, 113
Hergesheimer, Joseph, 15, 36, 59, 67, 70-72, 74, 92-93, 95, 118
Hibbens, John Grier, 32

Higgins, John A., 10-11, 55-58, 87-88, 94, 106, 111-112
Hindus, MIlton, 90, 112, 118
Hollywood story, 44, 55-57, 59, 74, 79, 81, 93, 104-108, 112
Hough, Emerson, 38
Hovey, Carl, 35-37
Howells, William Dean, 40
Huckleberry Finn, 61
Hughes, Langston, 84
"The Human Chase" (by Oppenheim), 60
Hunyady, Sandor, 108
Hussey, L. M., 19
In Our Time (by Hemingway), 50
"Introduction: Waltz: Coda" (by Hergesheimer), 92-93
"An Introductory Reminiscence," 19
irony, 26, 44, 58, 61, 68, 87, 99, 102, 107
James, Henry, 31
"jelly-bean," 27, 36, 41
"Jazz Age," spokesman for, 9, 31, 35-53, 83, 116, 118
Jones, Howard Mumford, 18
"Josephine Perry" stories, 67-69
Joyce, James, 18
Kazin, Alfred, 116, 118-119
Kelland, Clarence Budington, 40, 60, 74, 95
Kern, Jerome, 97
Kerr, Sophie, 63
Kipling, Rudyard, 13
Komroff, Manuel, 83, 108
"Korea's Rebellion: The Part Played by Christians," 31
Kuehl, John, 24
Ladies' Home Journal, 17, 43
Lardner, Ring, 15, 40, 77, 85
Lawrence, D. H., 85

The Last Laocoon (by Sklar), 29, 117
Leatherstocking-style heroes, 28
LeFevre, Edwin, 65
The Letters of H. L. Mencken, 17
Lewis, Sinclair, 15, 82
Liberty, 43, 48, 53, 74, 80-81, 86, 91, 94, 104
Lindsey, Ben B., 48
Littauer, Kenneth, 94-96
"Little Angevine" (by McFee), 84
"The Little Fellow on Wall Street" (by LeFevre), 65
"Little Orvie" series (by Tarkington), 92
"The Lively Arts" (by Seldes), 85
London, Jack, 15-16
"The Lonesome Vigilante" (by Steinbeck), 100
Long, Ray, 40
Lorimer, George Horace, 10-11, 14-15, 28-30, 38, 40, 44, 47, 53, 55-58, 62-64, 66, 72, 74, 91-94, 117
Lorimer, Graeme, 92
"Lost and Unpublished Stories by F. Scott Fitzgerald" (by Atkinson), 10, 94
Macfadden, Bernarr, 35-36, 81
Magazines in the United States (by Wood), 14
The Man Nobody Knows (by Barton), 48
"March family" series (by Marquand), 92
Marks, Percy, 67
Marquand, John P., 38, 62, 65, 67, 72, 74, 78-79, 92, 95
Marquis, Don, 63
Marshall, Marguerite Mooers, 43

Marx, Harpo, 86
Masters, Edgar Lee, 82, 86
"Matthewson" (by Dreiser), 83
Maugham, W. Somerset, 41
Maurois, André, 86
McCall's, 39, 43, 50, 81, 91, 94
McClure's, 15
McDougall, Joseph E., 100
McFee, William, 84
medical settings, 72-73, 79-81, 92-93, 97, 101-102
medieval romance, 80-81
Mencken, H. L., 9-10, 15-19, 21-25, 30, 37, 40, 43-44, 48, 52, 82, 84, 94, 116
"Merton of the Movies" (by Wilson), 38
The Metroplitan Magazine, 35-40
Millay, Edna St. Vincent, 18
Miller, Alice Duer, 79
Milne, A. A., 46
Mitchell, Margaret—SEE: *Gone With the Wind*
Mizener, Arthur, 31, 116
"modern" short story, 84, 97
Montaigne, Michel de, 23
Monteiro, George, 103
Moran, Lois, 57
"Murder on a Calais Coach" (by Christie), 79
Murder on the Orient Express (by Christie), 79
Mussolini, Benito, 67
"My War Dairy" (by Mussolini), 67
mystery genre, 46, 50, 56, 67, 79, 81, 92, 102
Nassau Literary Magazine, 13, 20
Nathan, George Jean, 16-21, 24-26, 37-40, 44, 82, 86, 90, 100, 108, 119
"The National Letters" (by Mencken), 15

naturalism, 18, 24, 37, 87, 116
Nazi Germany, 100
"Nero Wolfe" series (by Stout), 92
The New Republic, 77, 95
New York American, 43
The New Yorker, 65, 103
nineteenth century settings, 87
Norris, Frank, 15-16, 18
Norris, Kathleen, 40
Nothing But People (by Ginrich), 82
Ober, Harold, 15, 21, 26, 35-36, 38-41, 46-47, 52-53, 55, 62, 64-65, 68, 71, 74, 80, 88-92
The Octopus (by Norris), 15
"Oh, Major, Major" (by Marquand), 62
O'Neill, Eugene, 18, 21
"Only a Few of Us Left" (by Marquand), 38
Oppenheim, E. Phillips, 40, 60, 65
"Our American Women Are Leeches" (by Marshall), 43
Oursler, Charles Fulton, 36
pastoral theme, 21, 28
"Pat Hobby" stories, 104-108, 113-114
Payne, Will, 65
Perkins, Maxwell, 32, 62, 64, 81, 90, 102, 108, 113
Perosa, Sergio, 89-90, 105-107, 111-112, 118
Petty (illustrator), 109
"Phillipe" series, 80-81, 88, 104
Piper, Henry Dan, 19, 30, 36, 71, 73, 78, 88, 92-93, 95, 109, 118
Pirandello, Luigi, 86
The Pit (by Norris), 15
plot construction, 118
"The Poor Fish" (by Graeve), 56

129

Pound, Ezra, 82, 86, 90, 108
Prejudices, 15
Princeton Tiger, 21, 45
Princeton University, 13, 21, 32, 65, 91, 97, 101
Princeton University Library Chronicle, 13
Publishers Weekly, 9
"The Purple Palette of Life" (by Abdullah), 17
Queen, Ellery, 81
"Queen in the Parlor Car" (by McDougall), 100
Raine, Nelson Reilly, 92
"The Rape of Lucrece," 26
realism, 17, 19, 21, 111
Red Book, 16, 35, 46, 48-50, 73, 78, 80-81, 94, 96, 104, 118
regionalism, 28
"Repetition Generale," 18
Rinehart, Mary Roberts, 79, 95
Roaring Twenties, 9
Roche, Arthur Somers, 50, 81
"Romance" (by Child), 51
romance and romantic comedy, 18, 20, 26-30, 36-37, 41-42, 50-51, 56-58, 62, 81, 92-93, 95, 117
Roscoe, Burton, 85
Russell, Bertrand, 85
"Salute and Farewell to F. Scott Fitzgerald" (by Ginrich), 115
Saroyan, William, 86
"Sartoris" series (by Faulkner), 92
The Saturday Evening Post, 10-11, 14-15, 19, 23, 25-31, 33, 35-40, 43-48, 50-52, 55-75, 77-84, 87, 89, 91-96, 101-103, 107, 112-113, 117-119
Sayre, Zelda—SEE: Fitzgerald, Zelda Sayre

Scott Fitzgerald (by Turnbull), 57
screenwriting, 104
Scribner's Magazine, 31-33, 74, 80
"Second Choice" (by Alexander), 59
Seldes, Gilbert, 85
series characters, 92
Service, Robert, 13
Shakespeare, William, 25, 27
Shaw, George Bernard, 13
Shaw, Irwin, 108-109
sheiks, 50
"Shooting at the Moon" (by Campbell), 85
Sklar, Robert, 29-31, 52, 57, 60-61, 87, 117
Smart, David, 82
The Smart Set, 16-27, 29, 31, 33, 37, 39-40, 44, 63, 84-85, 100, 112, 116, 118
Smart Set: A History and Anthology (by Dolmetsch), 19
Smith, Thorne, 81
"The Snows of Kilimanjaro" (by Hemingway), 100
"The Sound and the Fury" (magazine column), 101-102
Spanish Civil War, 100
Spencer, Herbert, 31
"Squire Dinwiddy" (by Caldwell), 108
Steinbeck, John, 100
Stenerson, Douglas C., 18
Stock Market crash, 65, 70-71, 79
Stout, Rex, 92
Stout, Wesley Winans, 93
Street, Julian, 65
Stuart, Jesse, 100, 108
style, 118
supernatural, 58-59, 69, 102
Swanson, H. N., 49

"Sweet Faces and Foul Minds" (by Nathan), 86
Swinburne, Algernon Charles, 13, 16
Tarkington, Booth, 13, 60-62, 65, 67, 92, 95
Tarleton, Georgia stories, 27-28, 36, 41
Tebbel, John, 14-15, 38
"Thoughts on Being Bibliographed" (by Wilson), 13
"Thrift" (by Faulkner), 67
To Have and Have Not (by Hemingway), 100
"Todd's Plunge" (by Adams), 29
Tolstoi, Lev, 23
Tom Sawyer (by Twain), 61
Topper (by Smith), 81
Town and Country, 82
"The Tradesman's Return" (by Hemingway), 100
Train, Arthur, 27, 74
Triangle Club, 13
"trickster tricked," 27, 61, 105
Trotsky, Leon, 86
"Trouble" stories, 92
True Story, 36
"Tugboat Annie" series (by Raine), 92
Tully, Jim, 83
Turnbull, Andrew, 30, 57
"Two Sets of Books, One Balance Sheet: 'Financing Finnegan'" (by Monteiro), 103
"Up from Heaven" (by Chamberlain), 44, 56-57, 63
Upton, William Hazlett, 74
Van Dine, S. S., pseud. of Willard Huntington Wright, 16
Van Dyke, Henry, 31
van Saanen, Marie Louise, 17
Vanity Fair, 38, 82
Vargas (illustrator), 109

"Warning Hill" (by Marquand), 62
Weaver, John V. A., 85, 100
Weintraub, William 82
Weir, Charles, Jr., 119
Wells, H. G., 13, 41
West, James L. W. III, 97, 104
Wilde, Oscar, 13, 16, 20
Wiley, Hugh, 48, 60, 74
Williams, Ben Ames, 46
Wilson, Edmund, 9-10, 13, 20, 77, 116
Wilson, Harry Leon, 15, 38, 65
Winslow, Thyra Samter, 19
"Winter with the Cigales" (by Gray), 78
Woman's Home Companion, 43, 46-48, 94
Wood, James Playstead, 14
World War I, 14, 18-19, 23, 62, 67
World War II, 106
Wright, Austin McGiffert, 95, 117
Wright, Willard Huntington ("S. S. Van Dine"), 16
Yellow Nineties, 16
"Yes Sir; Thank You, Sir" (by Kerr), 63
"You, the Phantom" (by Dreiser), 86
Youmans, Vincent, 97
Zara, Louis, 108

STEPHEN W. POTTS

TITLE INDEX

"Absolution," 9, 43-44, 52
"The Adjuster," 48-49, 51-53
"The Adolescent Marriage," 51
"Afternoon of an Author," 98
"An Alcoholic Case," 101, 113
All the Sad Young Men, 37, 48, 52-53, 56
"The Ants of Princeton," 97, 113
As Ever, Scott Fitz—: Letters Between F. Scott Fitzgerald and His Literary Agent Harold Ober, 21-22, 26, 38-42, 47-48, 55, 59, 64-65, 68-69, 80, 92, 94
"At Your Age," 63-64
"Auction—Model 1934" (by Zelda Fitzgerald), 85
"Author" series, 97-99, 113
"Author's House," 97-98
"An Author's Mother," 98-99
"Babes in the Woods," 18-20, 22
"The Baby Party," 42, 46, 52
"Babylon Revisited," 9, 11, 69-72, 95
"Basil and Cleoptra," 62
"Basil Duke Lee" stories, 59-60, 62, 67, 95
The Beautiful and the Damned, 9, 25, 35, 37
"Benediction," 22, 30
"Bernice Bobs Her Hair," 27
"Between Three and Four," 70-71
"'Boil Some Water—Lots of It,'" 105
"A Book of One's Own," 103
"The Bowl," 59, 63
"The Bridal Party," 69
"The Camel's Back," 27
"The Captured Shadow," 61

"A Change of Class," 71-72
"The Count of Darkness," 81, 88
The Crack Up, 20, 116
"The Crack-Up" series, 89-90, 97-98, 107, 113-114
"Crazy Sunday," 9, 73-74, 79
"The Curious Case of Benjamin Button," 36, 39
"The Cut-Glass Bowl," 32
"Dalyrimple Goes Wrong," 22-23
"The Dance," 50
"Dearly Beloved," 110-111, 113
"The Debutante," 19-20, 22
"Design in Plaster," 104, 113
"Diagnosis," 72
"The Diamond as Big as The Ritz," 9, 25, 39-40, 52
"Diamond Dick and the First Law of Woman," 41
"Dice, Brass Knuckles, and Guitar," 41, 52-53
"Does a Moment of Revolt Come Sometime to Every Married Man?", 43
"Early Success," 103
"Echoes of the Jazz Age," 20, 74
"Emotional Bankruptcy," 68
"The End of Hate," 94, 104
"The Family Bus," 78
"Family in the Wind," 72-73
"The Far-Seeing Skeptics," 25, 38
"Fate in Her Hands," 91
"The Fiend," 87, 113
"Financing Finnegan," 102-103, 113
"First Blood," 67

Flappers and Philosophers, 115
"Flight and Pursuit," 71-72
"Forging Ahead," 61-62
"The Four Fists," 32
"A Freeze-Out," 72
"The Freshest Boy," 60-61
"Fun in an Artist's Studio," 105
"The Gods of Darkness," 81, 104
The Great Gatsby, 9-10, 35-36, 41-42, 44, 46, 50-53, 56-58, 69-70, 73, 80, 95, 112, 115, 119
"Gretchen's Forty Winks," 44-45, 51-52, 56-57
"The Guest in Room Nineteen," 102, 109, 113
"Gwen" stories, 91-92, 103
"Handle with Care," 89, 98, 107
"He Thinks He's Wonderful," 61
"Head and Shoulders," 26-27, 94
"Her Last Case," 79-80
"His Russet Witch," 36-37
"The Homes of the Stars," 105
"The Honor of the Goon," 101, 113
"Hot and Cold Blood," 41-42, 46, 52
"The Hotel Child," 69
"How to Live On Practically Nothing a Year," 45, 50-51
"How to Live On $36,000 a Year," 45
"How to Waste Material," 50
"'I Didn't Get Over,'" 99, 113
"I Got Shoes," 78
"The Ice Palace," 27-28, 36, 41
"Image on the Heart," 91
"Imagination—and a Few Mothers," 43

"In the Darkest Hour," 80-81
"In the Holidays," 102, 109, 113
"Indecision," 71
"Inside the House," 91
"The Intimate Strangers," 81
"Jacob's Ladder," 55-56, 63, 65
"The Jelly-Bean," 36-37, 41
"Jemima, the Mountain Girl," 38
"John Jackson's Arcady," 45-46, 55, 58
"Josephine Perry" stories, 67-69
"The Kingdom in the Dark," 81
"The Last of the Belles," 11, 62-63
The Last Tycoon, 9-10, 104, 111-112, 116
"The Lees of Happiness," 37, 49
The Letters of F. Scott Fitzgerald, 30, 32, 62, 88, 93-94, 96, 108-109, 112
"The Long Way Out," 101-102, 113
"The Lost Decade," 104, 113
"The Love Boat," 58
"Love in the Night," 50-51, 58
"Magnetism," 59
"Majesty," 63-64
"A Man in the Way," 105
"May Day," 24-25
"Mightier than the Sword," 105, 108
"A Millionaire's Girl" (by Zelda Fitzgerald), 68-69
"More Than Just a House," 78
"Mr. Icky: The Quintessence of Quaintness in One Act," 21-22, 38
"Myra Meets His Family," 26-27, 29
"A New Leaf," 71

133

"New Types," 79
"A Nice Quiet Place," 67-68
"A Night at the Fair," 60
"The Night before Chancellorsville," 87, 113
"No Flowers," 79
"No Harm Trying," 105
"Not in the Guidebook," 47
"O Russet Witch!," 36
"Obit on Parnassus," 103
"The Offshore Pirate," 28, 30, 42, 67, 94
"Offside Play," 94
"On an Ocean Wave" (by "Paul Elgin"), 109, 113
"On Schedule," 77
"On the Trail of Pat Hobby," 105, 108
"One Hundred False Starts," 77
"One Interne," 73, 77-78
"One of My Oldest Friends," 46-47
"One Trip Abroad," 69
"The Ordeal," 22
"Our Own Movie Queen" (with Zelda Fitzgerald), 50
"Outside the Cabinet-Maker's," 65, 112
"The Passionate Eskimo," 81, 88
"Pasting it Together, 89
"Pat Hobby and Orson Welles," 105
"Pat Hobby Does His Bit," 105
"Pat Hobby, Putative Father," 105
"Pat Hobby" stories, 104-109, 111, 113-114
The Pat Hobby Stories, 108
"Pat Hobby's Christmas Wish," 105
"Pat Hobby's College Days," 105
"Pat Hobby's Preview," 105
"Pat Hobby's Secret," 105-106

"A Patriotic Short," 105-106
"A Penny Spent," 50
"The Perfect Life," 61
"Philippe" stories, 80-81, 88, 104
"The Popular Girl," 38-39, 78
"Porcelain and Pink," 21
"Presumption," 51
"The Pusher-in-the-Face," 46, 52
"Rags Martin-Jones and the Prnce of W-les," 42, 51-52
"The Rich Boy," 9, 49-50, 52, 59, 112, 117
"Ring," 77
The Romantic Egoist, 13
"The Rough Crossing," 64
"The Rubber Check," 73
"The Scandal Detectives," 60
"'Send Me In, Coach,'" 99
"'The Sensible Thing,'" 42, 52
"Shaggy's Morning," 88, 113
The Short Stories of F. Scott Fitzgerald, 97, 103
"A Short Trip Home," 58-59
"'Show Mr. and Mrs. F. to Number—'" (by Zelda Fitzgerald), 83, 85
"Six of One—," 73
"Sleeping and Walking," 86, 89, 98
"The Smilers," 23-24, 37
"A Snobbish Story," 68
"Strange Sanctuary," 91-92, 103
"The Swimmers," 64-65
Tales of the Jazz Age, 22, 24-25, 36-37
Taps at Reveille, 64, 87-88
"Tarquin of Cheapside," 25, 38
"Teamed With Genius," 105
Tender Is the Night, 9-10, 57, 64, 66, 75, 80, 88, 93, 95, 112
"The Third Casket," 44-45, 52
"This Is a Magazine," 38

This Side of Paradise, 9, 13-15, 19-20, 23-25, 31-33, 45, 52, 60-61, 115-116
"Three Acts of Music," 97
"Three Hours Between Planes," 110, 113
"Thumbs Up," 94
"Too Cute for Words," 91
"Trouble" stories, 92, 101
"Two for a Cent," 37
"Two Old-Timers," 105
"Two Wrongs," 66
"The Unspeakable Egg," 45-46
The Vegetable, 35, 44
"Wait Till You Have Children of Your Own!", 43
"What a Handsome Pair!", 73
"What Became of Our Flappers and Sheiks?", 50
"What I Think and Feel at Twenty-Five," 40
"What Kind of Husbands Do 'Jimmies' Make?", 43
"What to Do About It," 78
"Who's Who—and Why," 31
"Why Blame It on the Poor Kiss if the Girl Veteran of Many Petting Parties Is Prone to Affairs After Marriage?", 43
"Winter Dreams, 36-37, 51-52, 110
"The Woman from Twenty-One," 110
"A Woman with a Past," 68
"Your Way and Mine," 47-48
"Zone of Accident," 81-82

CHARACTER INDEX

Abe, 99
Andy, 63
Ardita, 29, 42
Baker, Jordan, 113
Barton, Peter, 24
Basil—SEE: Lee, Basil Duke
Bernice, 27
Bibble, Minnie, 61-62
Bill, 58
Blaine, Amory, 13, 19-20
Blair, Hubert, 60
Booth, Jacob, 55
Bowman, Yanci, 38
Bradin, Edith, 24-25
Bradin, Henry, 24-25
Button, Benjamin, 39
Calhoun, Ailie, 63
Carraway, Nick, 113
Carroll, 24-25
Cory, Philip, 24
Crenshaw, 87
Dalyrimple, 22-23
Dean, Philip, 24
Delahanty, Jenny (i.e., "Jenny Prince"), 55
Diamond Dick, 41
Gatsby, Jay, 36, 113
George, 45
Green, Dexter, 36-37
Gus, 24-25
Gwen, 91-92, 106
Hannaford, George, 59
Happer, Sally Carol, 27-28
Harlan, Dolly, 59
Hibbing, 99
Himmel, Peter, 24
Hobby, Pat, 104-108
Horace, 26
Hoyt, Rosemary, 57
Hunter, Anson, 49
Isabelle, 19-20
Jackson, John, 46
Janney, Dr. Forrest, 72-73
Johnson, Hamilton T., 98-99
Jones, Judy, 36-37
Kellys, 69
Kimberly, Scott, 38
Lamar, Nancy, 36
Lee, Basil Duke, 59-62
Mae/May, 58
Marcia, 26
Marjorie, 27
Marston, Henry, 64-65
Martin-Jones, Rags, 42
McChesny, Bill, 66
Moran, Kieth, 22
Moran, Lois, 22
Moreland, Toby "Curtis Carlyle," 29
Mr. In and Mr. Out, 24
Myra, 26-27
Olive, 64
Palms, Stephen (i.e., Amory Blaine), 19-20
Paula, 49
Perry, Josephine, 67-69
Plant, Donald, 110
Powell, Jim, 36, 41
Ragland, Dick, 71
Roger, 44-45
Rosalind, 19
Smith, Adrian, 64
Smith, Dr. (i.e., Dr. Moon), 48-49
Smith, Eve, 64
Sterrett, Gordon, 24-25
Thorne, Vienna, 59
"Trouble," 92-93
Villfranche, Philippe de, 80-81, 104
Wales, Charlie, 69-70
Wales, Honoria, 69-70
Washington, Braddock, 40
Wiese, 65